50 YEARS

lonely 🌐 planet

OF TRAVEL

POCKET

HAVANA

TOP EXPERIENCES • LOCAL LIFE

T0067033

BRENDAN SAINSBURY

Capitolio Nacional (p70)
MARCO BORGHINI/SHUTTERSTOCK ©

Contents

Welcome to Havana

On first impression, Havana can seem like a confusing jigsaw puzzle, but work out how to put the pieces together and a beautiful picture emerges. Herein lies a world-class art culture, history piled up like hoarded treasure in a dusty attic, and an indefatigable salsa energy that ricochets off walls and emanates most emphatically from the people.

Catedral de la Habana (p38)
JAMES_GABBERT/GETTY IMAGES ©

Top Experiences

See five centuries of architecture in Plaza Vieja (p36)

Be dazzled by gold and marble at the Capitolio Nacional (p70)

Climb the ramparts of the Parque Histórico Militar Morro-Cabaña (p60)

Evoke the flavors of centuries past in Calle Mercaderes (p40)

Embrace the avant-garde at Fusterlandia (p128)

See Cuban painting at the Museo Nacional de Bellas Artes (p68)

Behold the baroque at the Catedral de la Habana (p38)

Walk the haunting lanes of the Necrópolis Cristóbal Colón (p90)

Decipher Havana's history at the Museo de la Ciudad (p42)

Sip a mojito in the Hotel Nacional (p92)

Explore a literary legacy at Museo Hemingway (p140)

Uncover Santería at the Iglesia de Nuestra Señora de Regla (p64)

Dining Out

Havana's eating scene has progressed exponentially since the early 2010s despite perennial difficulties in procuring ingredients. The most condensed scene is in Habana Vieja. Playa has the most exclusive restaurants. Culinary experimentation has also proliferated. You can now find Russian, Lebanese, Indian and Iranian restaurants.

Stewing 500 Years

Cuba's cuisine is a creative stew of selective morsels, recipes and cooking techniques left behind by successive travelers since the epoch of Columbus and Velázquez. Imagine a bubbling cauldron filled with ingredients plucked from Spain, Africa, France, pre-colonial Taínos, and cultures from various other islands in the Caribbean that has been left to intermingle and marinate for 500 years.

From the original Taínos came indigenous root vegetables such as yucca and sweet potato, and native fruits such as guava; from the Spanish came pork, rice, flavor-enhancing spices and different frying techniques; African slave culture brought plantains in their various guises along with *congrí* (rice and beans cooked together with spices in the same pot); while, from its island neighbors, Cuba shares the unmistakable taste of the Caribbean enshrined in *sofrito,* a base

sauce of tomatoes seasoned with onions, peppers, garlic, bay leaf and cumin.

Farm-to-Table Restaurants

Ajiaco Café The pride of Cojímar offers cooking classes and traditional dishes with ingredients gathered from a nearby farm. (p139)

Grados Small, high-quality place in Vedado with a personal touch and a strong connection to the local community. (p105)

El Cimarrón Afro-Cuban-themed social project in suburban Vedado. (p105)

JON ARNOLD IMAGES LTD/ALAMY STOCK PHOTO ©

Best Tapas

Toros y Tapas Focusing on all things Spain, including the best traditional tapas. (p121)

Lo de Monik Adds a distinctive Cuban twist to the famous Spanish food tradition. (p52)

Cheap & Quick

D'Next The living embodiment of the notion that sometimes simple (and speedy) is best. (p52)

Café Bohemia Sweet snacks and savory tapas as good as the bohemian atmosphere in Plaza Vieja. (p54)

El Biky Cool retro diner affiliated with Havana's

freshest, most aromatic bakery. (p103)

La Casa del Gelato The gelato revolution hits full throttle in Miramar in this clean-lined ice-cream parlor. (p121)

Fine Dining

Otramanera A mini culinary Garden of Eden hidden behind a tall fence in Miramar. (p113)

San Cristóbal Follow in the footsteps of *muchos* famous people, including President Obama. (p80)

La Guarida A culinary legend that once provided the backdrop for an Oscar-nominated movie. (pictured; p80)

International Flavors

Nero di Seppia Arguably the best Italian restaurant in Havana amid some strong competition. (p120)

Casa Miglis This Swedish place in Centro Habana is renowned for its meatballs and toast *skagen*. (p81)

Topoly Iranian restaurant on a wraparound porch in Vedado that tempts you with fabulous sticky cakes. (p105)

La Catrina This Mexican-themed establishment in Playa is still something of a rarity in Cuba. (p122)

Bar Open

Havana's bar and cafe scene is going through an interesting stage. Bland international franchises have yet to gain a foothold, but, with more freedom to engage in private business, local entrepreneurs are directing their creativity into a growing number of bohemian drinking holes embellished with off-the-wall art and live music.

Habana Vieja

Calle Obispo is a throbbing wall of music after dark, with live bands competing to outdo each other. Plaza Vieja has emerged as the liveliest of the four main squares for nightlife, with lounge bars playing trance music, while once-forgotten Plaza del Cristo is where boho-beatniks go to forget Hemingway and rediscover Charlie Parker reborn as a punk rocker. San Isidro is the latest emerging nightlife district.

Centro Habana

Centro Habana's nightlife has always been a bit more *caliente* than Habana Vieja's and decidedly more 'local' than Vedado's, with the streets here never lifeless. For a more sophisticated evening, hit a bar in one of the top-end hotels around Parque Central. The Hotel Packard's is exquisite.

Vedado

Vedado was the hot spot of Havana's nightlife even before the revolution, when the US Mafia controlled most of the nocturnal action. The variety of nighttime activities is huge and growing at a furious pace. Recent openings have included fancy clubs, beatnik cafes and cool cocktail bars.

Coffee

Café Arcángel Small, one-of-a-kind cafe in a tatty Centro Habana street. (p84)

Café Fortuna Joe Weirdest cafe in Havana – no contest. You can even imbibe your *cafecito* while sitting on a toilet seat! (p115)

El Café The best place in Havana to enjoy a cup of morning joe with a formidable breakfast. (p56)

Origenes Coffee and cake comes with a five-star ambience at this dessert buffet in Hotel Royalton Paseo del Prado. (p84)

Cafes Doubling as Art Galleries

Café Madrigal Weird, wacky and Warhol-esque fount of good cocktails and even better art. (p91)

Espacios Huge canvases offer talking points for cocktail-quaffing artists. (p115)

El Dandy Strong coffee, interesting people, head-turning wall art and top-notch service. (pictured, left; p55)

Iconic Bars

La Bodeguita del Medio Brave the chaos at this cradle of the mojito – and shrine to Hemingway. (pictured, right; p56)

El Floridita Get your photo taken next to a statue of Hemingway and sink an obligatory daiquiri. (p56)

Sloppy Joe's Don't worry: it's not at all sloppy and the owner is no longer called Joe. (p84)

Hotel Nacional Raise a toast with the ghosts of Churchill and Sinatra. (p92)

Places for Cocktails

Azúcar Lounge Poised like a theater box suspended above Plaza Vieja and offering great cocktails. (p55)

Malecón 663 Havana's one-stop shop for high culture. (p83)

El Bleco The trendiest perch in Havana to be seen with a mojito in your hand. (p83)

Bars with Live Music

Pazillo Bar Suave nexus for light bites, potent cocktails and gentle sounds in a handsome Vedado house. (p108)

El Antonia Restaurant that doubles up as a bar and becomes an intimate live music venue in the evenings. (p54)

Ley Seca Smooth jazz tests the acoustics in this speakeasy-themed bar in Habana Vieja. (p56)

Show Time

Although it may have lost its pre-revolutionary reputation as a casino quarter, Vedado is still the place for nightlife in Havana, with high-quality cabaret, jazz, classical music, dance and cinema on offer. Entertainment in Habana Vieja is emerging from a slumber and becoming more hip. Centro's nightlife is edgier and more local.

Into the Mix

Aside from the obvious Spanish and African roots, Cuban music has drawn upon a number of other influences. Mixed into an already exotic melting pot are genres from France, the US, Haiti and Jamaica. Conversely, Cuban music has also played a key role in developing various melodic styles and movements in other parts of the world. In Spain they called this process *ida y vuelta* (return trip) and it is most clearly evident in a style of flamenco known as *guajira*. Elsewhere the 'Cuban effect' can be traced back to forms as diverse as New Orleans jazz, New York salsa and West African Afrobeat.

Rumba

Raw, expressive and exciting to watch, Cuban rumba is a spontaneous and often informal affair performed by groups of up to a dozen musicians. Conga drums, claves, *palitos* (sticks), *marugas* (iron shakers) and *cajones* (packing cases) lay out the interlocking rhythms, while the vocals alternate between a wildly improvising lead singer and an answering *coro* (chorus).

Live Music

Fábrica de Arte Cubano A potluck of performance art, from male choirs to female jazz jams. (p106)

Teatro Karl Marx First-stop theater venue for touring and local bands. (p125)

Jazz Club la Zorra y El Cuervo The best live jazz in the capital. (p109)

Café Teatro Bertolt Brecht Where Havana's 'yoof' queue up on Wednesday nights to see live bands such as Interactivo. (p95)

ANTONY SOUTER/ALAMY STOCK PHOTO ©

Cabaret

Tropicana Nightclub It's expensive and there are lots of tourists, but that doesn't stop it being good. (p125)

Cabaret Parisién A thoroughly decent alternative to the Tropicana that kicks off nightly in the Hotel Nacional. (pictured; p109)

Habana Café Tourist-heavy cabaret in the Hotel Meliá Cohiba in a retro American setting. (p110)

Cabaret Las Vegas Havana's best LGBTIQ+ shows. (p108)

Son & Salsa

El Guajirito Dinner shows with retro Buena Vista Social Club music. (p86)

Sociedad Cultural Rosalia de Castro Old-timers belting out traditional music with the enthusiasm of 20-year-olds. (p86)

Bar-Restaurante 1830 After-dinner salsa dancing on the Malecón with water views. (p108)

Cinemas

Cine Yara Cuba's most famous cinema has a wide selection of international movies. (p95)

Cine Infanta Multiplex cinema that co-hosts the December film festival. (p86)

Cine Charles Chaplin Director's cuts, Chaplin features and a museum of film posters in the lobby. (p110)

Havana Festivals

Havana has a wealth of annual festivals. A top three would include the **Festival Internacional de Ballet de la Habana**, a biennial dance festival held in late October, the **Festival Internacional de Jazz**, hosted in January, and the widely lauded **Festival Internacional del Nuevo Cine Latinoamericano**, celebrating film in December.

Art & Architecture

EQROY/SHUTTERSTOCK ©

There is nothing pure about Havana's architecture. Rather like its music, the city's eclectic assemblage of buildings exhibits an unashamed hybrid of styles, ideas and influences. The result is a kind of architectural 'theme and variations' that has absorbed a variety of imported genres and shaped them into something uniquely Cuban.

Architectural Styles

Havana's classic and most prevalent architectural styles are baroque and neoclassicism. Baroque designers began sharpening their quills in the 1750s; neoclassicism gained the ascendancy in the 1820s and continued, amid numerous revivals, until the 1920s. Trademark buildings of the American era (1902–59) exhibited art deco and, later on, modernist styles. Art nouveau played a cameo role during this period, influenced by Catalan *modernisme;* art nouveau curves and embellishments can be seen on pivotal east–west axis streets in Centro Habana. Ostentatious eclecticism, courtesy of the Americans, characterized Havana's rich and growing suburbs from the 1910s.

Havana's Art

Havana isn't traditionally cited in the pantheon of great art cities alongside New York, Paris, Florence or Barcelona, but, arguably, it should be. An unconventional mix of Spanish classicism, European avant-gardism, primitivism and American modernism, developed for centuries in its own tropical setting, has endowed the capital with a unique and independent art culture.

Best Art

Fusterlandia A whole neighborhood covered in a giddy array of mosaics, tiles and bright paintings. (p128)

Fábrica de Arte Cubano Probing, cutting-edge, always surprising art unleashed in this unique art 'factory.' (p106)

Museo Nacional de Bellas Artes The whole history of Cuban art supported by a commendable

GIL.K/SHUTTERSTOCK ©

collection of international masterpieces. (p68)

Callejón de Hamel Cradle of Havana's Afro-Cuban culture and colorful exponent of street art. (pictured, right; p76)

Galería-Taller Gorría Inspiring gallery anchoring a community art district in Habana Vieja. (p55)

Architecture

Catedral de la Habana This curvaceous stone colossus is the pinnacle of Cuban baroque. (p38)

Plaza Vieja Havana's most multifarious square exhibits every architectural style from Mudejar to art nouveau. (p36)

Capitolio Nacional A towering example of

20th-century neoclassicism completely refurbished for Havana's 500th anniversary in 2019. (p70)

Edificio Bacardí One of the finest examples of art deco architecture in the Americas. (pictured, left; p51)

Hotel Nacional This turreted hotel is one of Havana's most emblematic buildings both inside and out. (p92)

Churches

Iglesia y Convento de Nuestra Señora de la Merced Havana's finest church interior is a riot of frescoes and gilded trimmings. (p51)

Iglesia Jesús de Miramar Worth a visit for both its architecture and art, especially its monumental stations of the cross. (p115)

Walking Tour

A great way to see Havana's art and architecture is with **Free Walking Tour Havana**. The wonderfully insightful tours kick off at the Plazuela de Santo Ángel at 9:30am and 4pm daily and last two to three hours. Reserve online or phone ahead. Tips are appreciated.

Under the Radar

Havana is a city of many layers and secrets: there's a rampant 'black' market, an ever-confusing juxtaposition of private and state-run business, and the complex syncretism of Santería, to name three examples. For the gist of what's going on, you need to dip under the radar and glimpse what locals call la lucha Cubana (the daily struggle).

Meet the Locals Over Ice Cream

During the day, the Coppelia park is characterized by its snaking lines of people, 99% of them Cuban. The fuss? Ice cream. Love affairs have been forged in these patient queues and the plot of Oscar-nominated film *Fresa y Chocolate* (Strawberry and Chocolate) hinged on a spontaneous Coppelia meeting in its alfresco ice-cream parlor. Park yourself at a communal table and it's pretty much guaranteed that you'll meet some interesting locals.

This Sporting Life

Sport is a great cultural leveler wherever you go, and no more so than in Cuba where attending a game costs next to nothing. The national sport is baseball and it's fiercely debated all day, every day at a noisy nexus in Parque Central known as the *esquina caliente* (hot corner). For a game featuring Havana's beloved Industriales, you'll need to get yourself to the Estadio Latinoamericano (Zequiera No 312, Cerro; tickets US$2) in the municipality of Cerro, just as President Obama did when he visited Cuba in March 2016 (the season runs August to January). Failing this, street baseball is everywhere. Walk down any *calle* in Centro Habana and you'll stumble upon numerous improvised diamonds.

Fun Alternatives

San Isidro Art District In a less-touristed section of Habana Vieja replete with urban graffiti, galleries and bars. (p55)

JEREMY GRAHAM/ALAMY STOCK PHOTO ©

Real Habana A private restaurant in Centro Habana where most of the clients are Cuban and the food is true to its roots. (p80)

Centro Cultural Antiguos Almacenes de Deposito San José Havana's largest private vendors' market is a mini-hive of *capitalismo*. (pictured; p58)

Centro Cultural Enguayabera Local cultural center hosting music and art in the housing projects of Alamar. (p139)

Gimnasio de Boxeo Rafael Trejo The apex of Havana's boxing scene is open for shows, training and talent-spotting. (p57)

Paseo Maritimo 1ra y 70 Blustery seaside promenade lined with a rambunctious cluster of beach-shack seafood restaurants and *mucho* dancing. (p115)

Worth a Trip: Santuario de San Lázaro

Tucked away in the unspectacular Havana suburb of Rincón, the **Sanctuary of San Lázaro** is one of the nation's most important pilgrimage sites. Dedicated to the patron saint of the poor and sick, the church is venerated by both Catholics and followers of Santería. In Afro-Cuban religions the miraculous *orisha* (deity), Babalú Ayé, is syncretized with San Lázaro. Depicted as an old man with a sackcloth and crutches, San Lázaro is said to harbor divine healing powers. On his feast day on December 17, thousands walk to the church (some crawling on their knees) to pray for respite from illness or to give thanks for cures.

Responsible Travel

JULIO RIVALTA/SHUTTERSTOCK ©

Positive, sustainable and feel-good experiences around the city.

Support Local

Casas Over Hotels & Resorts Casas particulares are privately run and by staying in one you'll be putting money directly into the pockets of hardworking Cuban people. You'll also be privy to an uncensored glimpse of life as Cubans live it.

Farm-to-Table Restaurants A growing number of Cuban restaurants are starting to follow a farm-to-table ethos by teaming up with local *fincas* (farms) for their produce and ingredients. At Ajiaco Café in Havana you can visit a local farm as part of a cooking class. (p139)

Community Projects Havana has a number of community projects that have revitalized urban areas with art, gastronomy and small business. Notable examples include the San Isidro Art District and the Callejón de los Peluqueros in Habana Vieja, and the Callejón de Hamel in Centro Habana.

Agropecuarios Havana's local-produce markets are called *agropecuarios* and all neighborhoods have at least one. Usually they ply a mix of private and state-produced goods. Listen out for the *pregones* (comic singsong offering of wares).

Organopónicos *Organopónicos* are Cuba's urban farms and there are many in Havana. One of the largest and most impressive is the 11-hectare Organopónico Vivero Alamar, founded in 1997 in a prefab housing project near Cojímar. Tours are offered.

On the Road

Day Trip to Las Terrazas Las Terrazas in Artemisa Province provided a blueprint for reforestation in the '60s, restoring hectares of denuded woodland to prevent ecological disaster. Today it's a Unesco Biosphere Reserve with a good tourist infrastructure. Only 55km west of Havana, it's an easy day trip.

Car-Pool in a Colectivo *Colectivos* are part of the culture in Cuba; shared taxis that take up to four people who split the cost. They run between most major neighborhoods and can work out cheaper than buses.

Go on a Bike Tour Several small private companies offer bike tours of Havana or will rent you a two-wheeled machine so you can sally forth

EDB3_16/GETTY IMAGES ©

independently. Ruta Bikes (rutabikes.com) and Havana Bikes (havana-bikes.com) are both recommended.

Car Ownership Cuba has one of the lowest rates of car ownership in the world, with 67 vehicles per 1000 people compared to 890 per 1000 in the US.

Give Back

Havana's Social Projects Join a social projects tour with Agencia de Viajes San Cristóbal in Havana and see how tourist money is reinvested back into the community by the City Historian's Office.

Resources

Complejo Las Terrazas lasterrazas.cu/en

Cubans in Defense of Animals (CeDA) cedacuba.org

City Historian's Office, Havana portal.ohc.cu

San Cristóbal travel agency, Havana viajes sancristobal.portal.ohc.cu

Climate Change & Travel

○ **It's impossible to ignore the impact** we have when traveling, and the importance of making changes where we can.

○ **Engage with your travel carbon footprint** There are many carbon calculators online that allow travelers to estimate the emissions generated by their journey; try resurgence.org/resources/carbon-calculator.html.

○ **Many airlines and booking sites offer travelers the option of offsetting** the impact of greenhouse gas emissions by contributing to climate-friendly initiatives around the world. We continue to offset the carbon footprint of all Lonely Planet staff travel, while recognising this is a mitigation more than a solution.

Treasure Hunt

THOMAS FRICKE/GETTY IMAGES ©

Sixty years of socialismo haven't done much for Havana's shopping scene. That said, there are some decent outlets for travelers, particularly for those seeking rum, cigars and coffee. Art is another worthwhile field: Havana's scene is cutting-edge and ever-changing, and browsers will find many galleries in which to while away the hours.

Cigars

La Casa del Habano Quinta The top choice of cigar aficionados has an affiliated bar and restaurant. (p126)

Casa del Habano – Hostal Conde de Villanueva Smoke shop in a historic Havana hotel known for its expert staff and rollers. (p59)

Real Fábrica de Tabacos Partagás Store Affiliated to Havana's famous tobacco factory, this shop specializes in the ultra-strong Partagás brand. (p58)

Art

Fusterlandia Several shops in the art district, including José Fuster's own studio, sell original work. (p128)

Centro Cultural Antiguos Almacenes de Deposito San José Numerous artists have stalls in Havana's largest private vendors' market. (p58)

Museo Nacional de Bellas Artes – Arte Cubano The museum shop has plenty of only-in-Cuba prints and drawings. (p69)

Private Shops

Memorias Librería Find antique collectibles in this jewel of an old book and magazine shop. (p87)

Clandestina Recycled clothes are the shape of things to come in this privately run boutique. (p57)

Librería Venecia Rare poster art, dog-eared books and the odd hidden treasure waiting to be found. (p58)

Local Specialties

Shops selling cigars, rum and coffee – Cuba's top three homegrown products – are relatively common in Havana. All are government-run. As a rule of thumb, never buy cigars off the street, as they will almost always be damaged and/or substandard.

Historic Sights

Havana is like a museum of museums, so numerous are its collected artifacts, from one of the best art galleries in the Caribbean to museums dedicated to coins, old playing cards and chocolate. Equally worth getting excited about are some magnificent forts, an eerily beautiful cemetery, and enough street art to fill a whole neighborhood.

ADWO/SHUTTERSTOCK ©

Historic Habana Vieja

In Havana, history is piled up like washed-up treasure on a tropical beach – except these days, thanks to the legacy of late City Historian Eusebio Leal Spengler, the colonial thoroughfares look a little less dusty. Leal helped nail Havana's exhausted infrastructure back together piece by piece for more than 30 years. The results are startling. Walk the streets of Habana Vieja today and you'll quickly feel a genuine connection with the past in imposing coastal fortifications and intimate, traffic-free plazas stuffed with museums.

Parque Histórico Militar Morro-Cabaña A two-fort complex and Unesco World Heritage site that's like a mini city armed to the hilt. (p60)

Castillo de la Real Fuerza Havana's oldest fort reflects on its history in a seafaring museum packed with scale models of grand old galleons. (pictured; p49)

Museo de la Ciudad The history of Havana laid out in one of its finest baroque buildings. (p42)

Plaza de la Catedral A textbook example of Cuban baroque architecture that hasn't changed much since the 18th century. (p39)

San Cristóbal Tours

Representing the Office of the City Historian, San Cristóbal offers a good selection of tours around the city's historic sights. Tours generally leave from 10am from the company's Habana Vieja office but always check ahead.

For Kids

Cubans love kids and kids invariably love Cuba. Welcome to a culture where children still play freely in the street. There's something wonderfully old-fashioned about kids' entertainment here, which is less about computer games and more about messing around with an improvised baseball bat and a rolled-up ball of plastic.

COLINMTHOMPSON/SHUTTERSTOCK ©

Planetario (Calle Mercaderes; ☎ 7-801-8544) Havana's planetarium includes a scale reproduction of the solar system inside a giant orb, a simulation of the Big Bang, and a theater that allows viewing of over 6000 stars. All pretty exciting stuff. It's only accessible by guided tours booked in advance. Tours take place Wednesday to Sunday and can be booked (in person) on Monday and Tuesday. (p37)

Fortaleza de San Carlos de la Cabaña Havana's ultimate fort has elongated ramparts, dozens of old weapons, horse-and-cart rides and a highly theatrical after-dark cannon-firing ceremony. (pictured; p61)

El Bosque de la Habana (Kohly) Includes a large kids' playground, ice-cream vendors, riverside walks and a large creeper-filled forest to spark the imagination. (p119)

Acuario Nacional (acuarionacional.cu/wifi; 🚻) Various reproductions of Cuba's coastal ecosystems, including a marine cave and a mangrove forest, can be found at the nation's main aquarium, in the Miramar district. (p117)

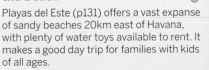

Fun on the Beach

Playas del Este (p131) offers a vast expanse of sandy beaches 20km east of Havana, with plenty of water toys available to rent. It makes a good day trip for families with kids of all ages.

LGBTIQ+

The Cuban LGBTIQ+ community's long road from marginalization to widespread acceptance was capped in 2022 when new laws recognizing same-sex marriage and adoption made it one of Latin America's most progressive states for LGBTIQ+ rights. Discrimination on the basis of sexual orientation and gender is now illegal.

NESTOR NOCI/SHUTTERSTOCK ©

It Started With a Film

The hit movie *Fresa y Chocolate* sparked the first national dialogue about homosexuality in Cuba soon after its release in 1994. The film tells the story of Diego, a skeptical homosexual artist who falls in love with a heterosexual communist militant who is secretly spying on him. It was nominated for an Oscar for best foreign language film and two of its main filming locations – the Coppelia and La Guarida restaurant – have become de rigueur sights in Havana.

LGBTIQ+ Locales

Cabaret Las Vegas Edgy local cabaret well-known for its drag shows. (p108)

Toke Infanta y 25 Gay-friendly cafe in the western reaches of Vedado that sells cheap snacks. (p105)

Café Cantante Mi Habana Rambunctious club in Cuba's National Theater complex with a Saturday night drag show. (p95)

Coppelia Made famous by *Fresa y Chocolate,* this ice-cream parlor and park are popular with the LGBTIQ+ crowd. (pictured; p95)

Hotel Telégrafo Axel Havana's erstwhile Telégrafo reopened as the city's first state-run LBGTIQ+ friendly hotel in Parque Central in 2022. (axelhotels.com/en/telegrafo-axel-hotel-la-habana/hotel.html)

Key Areas

The focus of Havana's gay life is on the border of Centro Habana and Vedado in the 'triangle' that stretches between Calzada de la Infanta, Calle L and Calle 23 (La Rampa).

Four Perfect Days

Day 1

KAMIRA/SHUTTERSTOCK ©

Explore Habana Vieja's four main colonial squares, stopping for coffee in **Plaza Vieja** (p36) and soaking up the atmosphere on shop- and museum-lined **Calle Mercaderes** (p40). Cut through tree-filled **Plaza de Armas** (p49), with its baroque palaces and Renaissance fort, on your way to the whimsical **Catedral de la Habana** (p38).

Get to grips with Havana's art culture by visiting the Cuban collection of the **Museo Nacional de Bellas Artes** (p68). Afterwards, walk down the Prado avenue and turn left into the **Malecón** (pictured; p73) sea drive to take in the sunset.

For Havana's trendiest after-dark quarter, head to the **Plaza del Cristo** (p51), where live music pulsates in cool bars.

Day 2

EGOROV ARTEM/SHUTTERSTOCK ©

Start with coffee in the **Plazuela de Santo Ángel** (p49). It's a short hop to the **Museo de la Revolución** (pictured; p87), encased in the Presidential Palace. After perusing the large outdoor exhibits, proceed to **Parque Central** (p78) and catch the **Habana Bus Tour** (p146) to Vedado.

Disembark near the **Universidad de la Habana** (p100), which has two small on-site museums. Nearby is the plusher **Museo Napoleónico** (p98), an ode to the erstwhile French emperor. Afterwards, wander over to the **Coppelia** (p95) for an ice cream.

Sip a mojito on the terrace at the **Hotel Nacional** (p92) and buy an evening ticket for the famous on-site **Cabaret Parisién** (p109).

Day 3

NIXY JUNGLE/SHUTTERSTOCK ©

Take a guided tour of the **Capitolio Nacional** (p70) and then dip into the lobbies of nearby historic hotels. Wise up on the Santería religion in the **Asociación Cultural Yoruba de Cuba** (p79) and join a tour around the neobaroque **Gran Teatro de la Habana Alicia Alonso** (pictured; p76).

Catch a bus or take a taxi to the **Museo Hemingway** (p140). Continue the Hemingway theme by squeezing into **La Bodeguita del Medio** (p56) for an obligatory mojito.

Head over to the **Fortaleza de San Carlos de la Cabaña** (p61) for the famous **cañonazo ceremony** (p62) at 9pm. Afterwards, return to Habana Vieja and wander the atmospheric streets in search of drinks and music.

Day 4

Head out to the western end of Playa and visit **Fusterlandia** (p128). On the way back, get a taxi to drop you off on the broad **Quinta Avenida**. Admire the eclectic mansions, many of them now embassies.

Cross over the Río Almendares in Vedado, perhaps stopping briefly in **El Bosque de la Habana** (p126). Head up Calle 23 to Havana's magnificent cemetery, the **Necrópolis Cristóbal Colón** (p90), which is particularly beautiful around sunset. If there's time, walk over to the **Plaza de la Revolución** (pictured; p99) and the **Memorial a José Martí** (p99).

Warm up with cocktails at **Café Madrigal** (p91) and spend the rest of evening at the incomparable **Fábrica de Arte Cubano** (p106).

Need to Know

For detailed information, see Survival Guide (p143)

Currency
Cuban peso (CUP$)

Language
Spanish

Money
Cuba is primarily a cash economy. Credit cards are used in state-run hotels and businesses. ATMs are widely available and accept some debit/credit cards.

Cell Phones
Check with your service provider to see if your phone will work (GSM or TDMA networks only). You can pre-buy services from the state-run phone company, Cubacel.

Time
Eastern Standard Time (GMT/UTC minus five hours)

Tipping
Wages in Cuba are low, and a tip can make a huge difference: 10% minimum; 15–20% for good service.

Daily Budget

Budget: Less than US$100
Room at a casa particular: US$30–50
Meal at a government-run restaurant: US$8–12
Cheap museum entry: US$1

Midrange: US$100–200
Room in a midrange hotel: US$50–120
Meal in a private restaurant: US$12–20
Mojito: US$3–4

Top end: More than US$200
Room in a historic hotel: US$200–325
City taxi: US$5–10
Tropicana cabaret: US$75

Advance Planning

Three months before Check visa requirements (especially if you're American), plan a general itinerary, book flights.

One month before Book hotels through travel agencies and/or email casa particular owners regarding availability. Check with your bank to see if your ATM cards will work. Check that the tourist card is included with your flight package.

72 hours before Fill out your obligatory D'Viajeros (travel form) online information form (dviajeros.mitrans.gob.cu).

Arriving in Havana

Havana is home to Cuba's main airport, Aeropuerto Internacional José Martí, 20km southwest of the city center. Almost all international visitors arrive by air.

The main bus company is Víazul. Services depart from a terminal 3.5km from central Havana. Víazul buses run from Havana to practically every city and town in Cuba of interest to tourists.

✈ From Aeropuerto Internacional José Martí

A standard taxi to central Havana will cost approximately US$30 (30 to 40 minutes).

🚌 From Terminal de Ómnibus

Taxis charge around US$5 for the short ride from the bus terminal to central Havana, or it's walkable if you have a light pack.

Getting Around

🚲 Bike

Two-seater bici-taxis will take you anywhere around Centro Habana for the equivalent of US$1 for a short trip, after bargaining.

⛴ Boat

A regular passenger ferry crosses the harbor between Habana Vieja and Habana del Este, Regla and Guanabacoa.

🚌 Bus

A tourist bus called Habana Bus Tour runs on two routes between 9am and 6pm and covers the main tourist sights. Crowded metro buses serve more peripheral neighborhoods on 16 routes.

🚗 Taxi

Taxis are ubiquitous, relatively cheap and go to areas that buses don't reach, especially in outer Havana.

Havana Neighborhoods

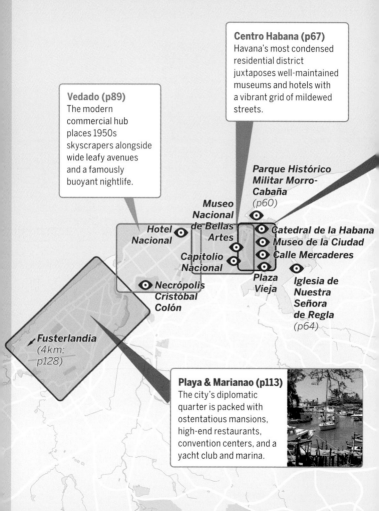

Centro Habana (p67)
Havana's most condensed residential district juxtaposes well-maintained museums and hotels with a vibrant grid of mildewed streets.

Vedado (p89)
The modern commercial hub places 1950s skyscrapers alongside wide leafy avenues and a famously buoyant nightlife.

Parque Histórico Militar Morro-Cabaña
(p60)

Museo Nacional de Bellas Artes

Hotel Nacional

Catedral de la Habana

Museo de la Ciudad

Calle Mercaderes

Capitolio Nacional

Plaza Vieja

Iglesia de Nuestra Señora de Regla
(p64)

Necrópolis Cristóbal Colón

Fusterlandia
(4km; p128)

Playa & Marianao (p113)
The city's diplomatic quarter is packed with ostentatious mansions, high-end restaurants, convention centers, and a yacht club and marina.

Habana Vieja (p35)
Thanks to a meticulous restoration program, Havana's original colonial core is crammed with well-preserved historical relics.

Playas del Este (p131)
The eastern coastal strip contains a succession of idyllic beaches, several all-inclusive hotels and the ocean-side Cuban village of Guanabo.

❯ *Museo Hemingway*
(p140)

Explore
Havana

Callejón de Hamel (p76) KAKO ESCALONA/GETTY IMAGES ©

Explore ⊕
Habana Vieja

Havana's Old Town is one of the historical highlights of Latin America; an architectural masterpiece where fastidiously preserved squares and grandiose palaces sit alongside a living, breathing urban community still emerging from decades of economic austerity. The result is by turns grand and gritty. No one should leave Cuba without seeing it.

The Short List

○ **Plaza Vieja (p36)** *Finding history, fine cafes and beauty in Habana Vieja's most multifarious square.*

○ **Catedral de la Habana (p38)** *Visiting Havana's main church and the pinnacle of Cuban baroque architecture.*

○ **Calle Mercaderes (p40)** *Walking in colonial footsteps in the restored confines of Havana's most historically authentic street.*

○ **Museo de la Ciudad (p42)** *Getting to grips with Havana's swashbuckling history in the entrails of its finest baroque palace.*

○ **Plaza del Cristo (p51)** *Plugging into Havana's bohemian grapevine in the city's artiest plaza.*

Getting There & Around

🚌 Metro buses run from the train station to Vedado and Playa. The Habana Bus Tour T1 bus stops at various places in Habana Vieja (including Plaza de Armas).

⛴ Small passenger ferries run to Casablanca and Regla on the eastern side of Havana's harbor.

🚕 A taxi to/from the airport takes around 40 minutes.

Habana Vieja Map on p46

Catedral de la Habana (p38) VADIM_N/SHUTTERSTOCK ©

Top Experience

See Five Centuries of Architecture in Plaza Vieja

Laid out in 1559, Plaza Vieja (Old Square) is Havana's most architecturally eclectic plaza, where Cuban baroque nestles seamlessly next to Gaudí-inspired art nouveau. Originally called Plaza Nueva (New Square), it was used for military exercises and later served as an open-air marketplace. Unlike other squares, Plaza Vieja is purely residential.

MAP P46, D6

Palacio Cueto

The distinctive Palacio Cueto (pictured), at the southeastern corner of the square, is Havana's finest example of art nouveau. Its ornate facade, dating from 1906, once fronted a warehouse and a hat factory before the building was rented by José Cueto in the 1920s as the Palacio Vienna hotel. It lay empty from the early 1990s, reopening in 2019 as a 60-room state-run hotel.

Palacio de los Condes de Jaruco

At the square's southwestern corner, Palacio de los Condes de Jaruco was constructed in 1738 from local limestone in a transitional Mudejar-baroque style. This muscular mansion is one of Plaza Vieja's oldest. Rich in period detail, it is typical of merchant houses of the era. For many years it was the residence of the exalted counts of Jaruco. Today it's the headquarters of Cuba's main cultural foundation. It underwent a lengthy restoration in the early 2020s.

The Fountain

A fountain has anchored the square since the 18th century and was originally fashioned in Carrara marble by Italian sculptor Giorgio Massari. It was (shamefully) demolished in the 1950s to make way for an underground car park, but a replica of the fountain was installed in the early 2010s. For a while it was surrounded by a black fence, supposedly to stop local schoolchildren jumping in it. The fence has been removed and the kids still play rambunctiously nearby.

★ Top Tips

o Plaza Vieja is a decent eating and drinking option; it has some attractive spots for coffee or a cocktail and is one of Habana Vieja's better corners for nighttime action.

o Other attractions on the square worth a look include a camera obscura and a planetarium.

o Look out on the western side of Plaza Vieja for some of Havana's finest *vitrales* (stained-glass windows) adorning the upper floors of a line of restored mansions. Semicircular *vitrales* were designed to colorfully refract the Caribbean sunshine and are a distinctive feature of Havana's colonial architecture.

✕ Take a Break

To survey the plaza's action, climb up for a theater-box view from Azúcar Lounge (p55).

For more intimacy, head under the arches to Café Bohemia (p54).

Habana Vieja See Five Centuries of Architecture in Plaza Vieja

Top Experience 📷

Behold the Baroque at the Catedral de la Habana

Dominated by two unequal towers and framed by a theatrical baroque facade designed by Italian architect Francesco Borromini, Havana's incredible cathedral was once described by novelist Alejo Carpentier as 'music set in stone.' The Jesuits began construction of the church in 1748 and work continued despite their expulsion in 1767. The church was finally consecrated in 1789.

◉ MAP P46, D3

Front Facade

The cathedral's unusual swirling facade is considered to be the apex of baroque architecture in Cuba. Although visually arresting and unique, the exterior walls were not as lavishly decorated as those of similar churches in Europe. This is due primarily to the hardness of the local limestone, but the lack of skilled craftspeople in 18th-century Cuba also played a role. Look closely and you'll see marine fossils embedded in the walls and pillars.

Interior

In contrast to its ornate facade, the cathedral's interior is neoclassical rather than baroque and relatively austere, the result of puritanical remodeling by an early-19th-century bishop. There are original Italian frescoes above the altar; the less valuable oil canvases that adorn the side walls are copies of works by Bartolomé Esteban Murillo and Peter Paul Rubens. You can climb the smaller of the cathedral's towers for a small fee.

Plaza de la Catedral

The cathedral is ringed by Cuba's most intimate and homogeneous square, a veritable museum to Cuban baroque, with all the surrounding buildings dating from the 1700s. Of particular note is the **Palacio de los Marqueses de Aguas Claras** on the western side, a majestic one-time palace completed in 1760 that features a beautiful, shady Andalucian patio (nowadays it houses a state-run restaurant). Another beauty is the **Palacio de los Condes de Casa Bayona** (directly opposite the cathedral), the square's oldest building, dating from 1720. Today it's occupied by the **Museo de Arte Colonial**.

★ **Top Tips**

○ Dress appropriately for the church: no sleeveless tops or micro-shorts.

○ Return to the square at night, when it has a totally different (and more intimate) atmosphere.

○ Some of Habana Vieja's best restaurants line a small alley (Callejón del Chorro) just off Plaza de la Catedral.

○ Listen out for word of classical-music concerts that are sometimes held in the square.

✕ **Take a Break**

One of the finest exponents of *comida criolla* (traditional Cuban food), Doña Eutimia (p52) is located in a cul-de-sac just off the square's southwestern corner, as are several other great restaurants.

Two blocks from the cathedral, El Rum Rum de la Habana (p52) is one of the city's suavest and most sophisticated restaurants.

Top Experience 📷
Evoke the Flavors of Centuries Past in Calle Mercaderes

Cobbled, car-free Calle Mercaderes (Merchants' St) has been extensively restored by the Office of the City Historian and is an almost complete replica of its splendid 18th-century high-water mark. Interspersed with the museums, shops and restaurants are some working social projects, such as a maternity home and a papermaking cooperative.

⊙ MAP P46, D4

Free Museums

Most of the myriad museums are free, including the **Casa de Asia**, with paintings and sculpture from China and Japan, the **Armería 9 de Abril**, an old gun shop (now museum) stormed by revolutionaries on the said date in 1958; and the **Museo de Bomberos**, which has antediluvian fire equipment dedicated to 19 Havana firefighters who lost their lives in an 1890 railway blaze.

Casa de África

Just off Mercaderes down Obrapía, it's worth slinking into the gratis Casa de África, which houses sacred objects relating to Santería and the secret Abakuá fraternity collected by ethnographer Fernando Ortíz.

An International Flavor

The corner of Mercaderes and Obrapía has an international flavor, with a bronze **statue** of Latin America liberator Simón Bolívar; across the street you'll find the **Museo de Simón Bolívar**, dedicated to Bolívar's life. The **Casa de México Benito Juárez** exhibits Mexican folk art and plenty of books but not a lot on Juárez (Mexico's first indigenous president) himself. Just east is the **Casa Oswaldo Guayasamín**, now a museum but once the studio of the great Ecuadorian artist who painted Fidel Castro in numerous poses.

Shops

Mercaderes is also characterized by its restored shops, including a perfume store, a spice shop and one of the city's best tobacco stores encased in the beautifully reimagined **Hostal Conde de Villanueva**. Wander at will.

★ **Top Tips**

○ Check out **Ediciones Boloña**, a small bookshop on the corner of Mercaderes and Obispo that sells books published or sponsored by the Office of the City Historian. Most are in Spanish and track the astounding renovation of Habana Vieja, illustrated with excellent photos.

○ Most of the street's museums open from 10am to 6pm Monday to Saturday, and until 1pm on Sunday.

✕ **Take a Break**

Several of Havana's top restaurants line Mercaderes, including elegant Paladar Los Mercaderes (p52). For a quicker, sweeter stop, hit the Museo del Chocolate (p57) for a mug of the hot sweet stuff.

Top Experience 📷

Decipher Havana's History at the Museo de la Ciudad

◉ MAP P46, D4

Even with no artifacts, Havana's city museum would be a tour de force, courtesy of the opulent palace in which it resides. Filling the whole western side of Plaza de Armas, the Palacio de los Capitanes Generales dates from the 1770s and is a textbook example of Cuban baroque, hewn out of rock from the nearby San Lázaro quarries. Huge rooms guard equally huge exhibits.

Changing Functions

From 1791 until 1898 the palace was the residence of the Spanish 'captains general,' the colony's administrative rulers. Then, for a brief period between 1899 and 1902, US military governors were based here. During the first two decades of the 20th century the building briefly became the presidential palace and, later, Havana's City Hall. The museum was created in 1968 after the palace became one of the first buildings in Habana Vieja to be renovated by Eusebio Leal, the City Historian. A life-sized statue of Leal, who died in 2020, stands in the street outside.

The Parroquia Mayor

The site on which the museum now stands was once occupied by Havana's main church, the Parroquia Mayor, built in the 1550s. The church was severely damaged when a ship blew up in Havana harbor in 1741 and was never repaired. Ultimately replaced by Havana's new Jesuit-built cathedral, it was finally demolished in 1771 to make way for the current palace. One room in the museum contains a collection of objects and vessels rescued from the original building.

Best Exhibits

The museum is wrapped regally around a splendid central courtyard adorned with a white-marble statue of Christopher Columbus (1862). Its artifacts (some of them a tad dusty) include period furniture, military uniforms and antique horse carriages. The real history-defining highlights are the boat used by Antonio Maceo to cross the Trocha de Mariel in 1896, a cannon captured by Independence War soldiers from the Spanish in 1897, and Cuba's first flag, raised by Narciso López in Cárdenas in 1850.

★ Top Tips

○ Audio guides are available in Spanish and English for a small cost.

○ Spare some time to visit the almost-as-opulent **Segundo Cabo** building on the north side of Plaza de Armas.

✕ Take a Break

Slip up Calle O'Reilly for some drinks and tapas at the ever-popular **O'Reilly 304** (📞5-264-4725) or its culinary cousin **El del Frente** (📞7-863-0206) on the rooftop across the street.

Habana Vieja Decipher Havana's History at the Museo de la Ciudad

Walking Tour 🥾

Rehabilitated Habana Vieja

The piecing together of Habana Vieja began in the late 1970s and is ongoing. The project, run by the Office of the City Historian, has restored Havana's most important historic buildings, created groundbreaking social projects for the local population, and garnered numerous international prizes for its cultural, historical and sustainable work.

Walk Facts

Start Casa de la Obra Pía
End Galería-Taller Gorría
Length 2km; one to two hours

❶ Casa de la Obra Pía

An architectural highlight in Habana Vieja is the Casa de la Obra Pía, originally a Spanish nobleman's mansion. The house was rehabilitated in 1983 as a museum and community project. The rooms facing Calle Mercaderes usually host revolving art exhibitions.

❷ Iglesia y Monasterio de San Francisco de Asís

Built in 1608, Iglesia y Monasterio de San Francisco de Asís ceased to have a religious function in the 1840s. Crypts and religious objects were dug up during excavations in the 1980s, and many of them are contained in the **Museo de Arte Religioso** that opened on the site in 1994.

❸ Angela Landa School

Plaza Vieja is perhaps the City Historian's most beautifully restored square, but it's not all for tourists. On its northern side is the Angela Landa school, which occasionally uses the square as a substitute playground and alfresco classroom. You'll see students running, playing sports, or sitting and reading beneath the giant *portales* (galleried walkways).

❹ Museo de la Farmacia Habanera

The wonderful art nouveau Sarrá pharmacy was founded by a Catalan immigrant in 1888. Restored in the 1990s, it functions as a pharmaceutical museum and a working pharmacy for the local population, selling mainly homeopathic products.

❺ Iglesia y Convento de Nuestra Señora de Belén

The huge 18th-century Iglesia y Convento de Nuestra Señora de Belén was restored by the City Historian in the 1990s, turning the building into an active community center. There are 18 permanent apartments for seniors, plus a sporadically open meteorology museum.

❻ San Isidro Art District

The grid of streets south of Calle Acosta was designated a special art district in the mid-2010s, with murals, galleries and regular events inspired by a mix of entrepreneurs and the Office of the City Historian. Center of operations is the Galería-Taller Gorría (p55), owned by Cuban actor Jorge Perugorría, and the affiliated bar/restaurant Yarini (p52).

Habana Vieja

For reviews see
- ⊙ Top Experiences p36
- ⊙ Sights p48
- ⊗ Eating p51
- ⊗ Drinking p55
- ⊙ Entertainment p57
- ⊙ Shopping p57

CASABLANCA

Fortaleza de San Carlos de la Cabaña

Bahía de la Habana

Castillo de San Salvador de la Punta
5

Parque Mártires del 71

Cárcel

Malecón
San Lázaro

Genios

Refugio

Colón

Trocadero

Animas

Paseo de Martí (Prado)

Agramonte

Av de las Misiones

San Juan de Dios

Edificio Bacardí 10

Plaza 13 de Marzo

Café del Ángel Jacqueline Fumero

Plazuela de Santa Ángel 6

Chacón 19

Aguacate

Compostela

Habana 22

Tejadillo

Empedrado 41

O'Reilly

Cuba

Aguiar 20

27

Cuarteles 23

Callejón de los Peluqueros 8

LOMA DEL ÁNGEL 32

21 13

Aguiar

Tacón

Parque Maestranza

Av Carlos Manuel de Céspedes

San Ignacio

29

Catedral de la Habana

Castillo de la Real Fuerza

Tacón

Palacio del Segundo Cabo 42

Callejón del Chorro

35 16

14

Museo de la Ciudad

Museo El Templete

Obispo 48
Justiz

Oficios 50

Calle Mercaderes 45

Museo Universitario 3

Calle Obispo

Cuba

Aguia

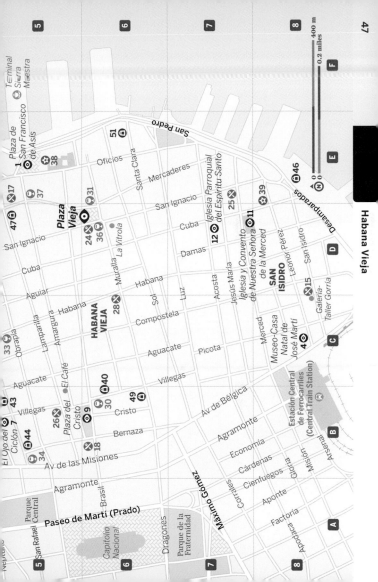

Habana Vieja

Terminal
Sierra
Maestra

Plaza de
San Francisco
de Asís

Plaza Vieja

HABANA
VIEJA

SAN
ISIDRO

Estación Central
de Ferrocarriles
(Central Train Station)

Parque
Central

Capitolio
Nacional

Parque de
la Fraternidad

Paseo de Martí (Prado)

Máximo Gómez

San Pedro

Oficios
Santa Clara
Mercaderes
San Ignacio
Cuba
Damas
Habana
Luz
Sol
Compostela
Aguacate
Picota
Villegas
Av de Bélgica
Agramonte
Economía
Cárdenas
Cienfuegos
Corrales
Aponte
Factoría
Apodaca

Desamparados
San Isidro
Leonor Pérez
Galería-
Taller Gorría
Merced
Misión
Gloria
Arsenal

Iglesia Parroquial
del Espíritu Santo
Iglesia y Convento
de Nuestra Señora
de la Merced
Museo-Casa
Natal de
José Martí

Jesús María
Acosta

La Vitrola
Muralla
Amargura
Habana
Lamparilla
Aguiar
Obrapía
El Café
Plaza del
Cristo
Cristo
Bernaza
Av de las Misiones
Agramonte
Brasil
Dragones

El Ojo del
Ciclón 7

San Rafael

Neptuno

400 m
0.2 miles

Sights

Plaza de San Francisco de Asís SQUARE

1  MAP P46, E5

Facing Havana harbor, the breezy Plaza de San Francisco de Asís first grew up in the 16th century when Spanish galleons stopped quayside on their passage from the Caribbean to Spain. A market took root in the 1500s, followed by a church in 1608, though when the monks complained about noise, the market was moved south to Plaza Vieja.

Museo Universitario MUSEUM

2  MAP P46, D4

This expertly curated museum tells the story of the numerous institutions that once stood on this site on Calle Mercaderes, from the erstwhile Convento de San Juan de Letrán, established in 1570, to the Dominican-run University of Havana, which welcomed students between 1728 and 1902 before moving to Vedado. The contemporary building was constructed over the skeleton of an ugly 1950s office block.

Calle Obispo STREET

3  MAP P46, D4

Narrow, chockablock Calle Obispo (Bishop's St) Habana Vieja's main interconnecting artery, is packed with art galleries, shops, music venues and people. Four- and five-story buildings block out most of the sunlight, and the swaying throng seems to move in time to the beautiful din

Castillo de San Salvador de la Punta

Plaza de Armas

Havana's oldest square was laid out in the early 1520s and today its impressive baroque facades harbor some of Havana's best museums.

Aside from the obligatory Museo de la Ciudad (p42), you should find time to admire the **Castillo de la Real Fuerza** (Map p46, E3), one of the oldest surviving forts in the Americas and host to the seafaring Museo de Navegación. Nearby, the chunky **Palacio del Segundo Cabo** (Map p46, D4; 🏛) is home to a museum dedicated to Cuban-European cultural relations, while the tiny **Museo El Templete** (Map p46, E3) marks the spot where Havana was founded in 1519 under a ceiba tree.

of competing live music that wafts out of the surrounding bars.

Museo-Casa Natal de José Martí   MUSEUM

4 👁 MAP P46, C8

Opened in 1925, this tiny museum, set in the house where the apostle of Cuban independence was born on January 28, 1853, is considered to be the oldest in Havana. The Office of the City Historian took the house over in 1994, and its succinct stash of exhibits devoted to Cuba's national hero continues to impress.

Castillo de San Salvador de la Punta   FORT

5 👁 MAP P46, B1

One in a quartet of forts defending Havana harbor, La Punta was designed by Italian military engineer Bautista Antonelli and built between 1589 and 1600. It underwent comprehensive repairs after the British shelled it during their successful 1762 Havana raid.

During the colonial era a chain was stretched 250m to the castle of El Morro (p61) every night to close the harbor mouth to shipping.

Plazuela de Santo Ángel   PLAZA

6 👁 MAP P46, B3

This lovely, intimate plaza behind the **Iglesia del Santo Ángel Custodio** has benefited from a community-driven beautification project that has installed several private restaurants, along with a statue of the fictional heroine Cecilia Valdés, who is watched over by a bust of the author who created her, Cirilo Villaverde.

El Ojo del Ciclón   GALLERY

7 👁 MAP P46, B5

Just when you think you've seen Havana's strangest, most surreal and avant-garde art, along comes the 'eye of the cyclone' to re-stretch your imagination. The abstract gallery displays the work of Cuban

Historical Jigsaw

Never in the field of architectural preservation has so much been achieved by so many with so few resources. You hear plenty in the international press about the sterling performance of the Cuban education and health-care systems but relatively little about the remarkable work that has gone into preserving the country's valuable, though seriously endangered, historical legacy, most notably in Habana Vieja.

A work in progress since the late 1970s, the piecing back together of Havana's Old Town after decades of neglect has been a foresighted and miraculous process, considering the economic odds stacked against it. The genius behind the project was Eusebio Leal Spengler (1942–2020), Havana's late City Historian, who, unperturbed by the tightening of the financial screws during Cuba's Special Period, in 1994 set up Habaguanex, a holding company that earns hard currency through tourism. The money Habaguanex grosses is reinvested in the city, shared between historical preservation (to attract more tourists) and citywide urban regeneration (to benefit ordinary *habaneros*).

Eschewing the temptation to turn Havana's old quarter into a historical theme park, Leal sought to rebuild the city's urban jigsaw as an authentic 'living' center that provides tangible benefits for the neighborhood's 82,000-plus inhabitants. As a result, schools, neighborhood committees, care homes for seniors and centers for children with disabilities sit alongside cleaned-up colonial edifices. Every time you put your money into a Habana Vieja hotel, museum or restaurant, you are contributing not just to the quarter's continued restoration but to a raft of projects that directly benefit the local population.

Today, the Office of the City Historian splits its annual tourist income (reported to be in excess of US$160 million) between further restoration (45%) and social projects in the city (55%), of which there are now more than 400. So far, one quarter of Habana Vieja has been returned to its colonial-era splendor, with tourist attractions including 20 Habaguanex-run hotels, four classic forts and over 30 museums.

artist Leo D'Lázaro and it's pretty mind-bending stuff – giant eyes, crashed cars, painted suitcases and junk reborn as art. Imagine Jackson Pollock sitting down for tea with JRR Tolkien and John Lennon. (📞7-861-5359)

Callejón de los Peluqueros

STREET

8 📍 MAP P46, C2

The brainchild of barber Gilberto Valladares, aka 'Papito,' this revitalized community project is based upon a novel hairdressing salon that doubles up as a school and small museum to the barber's art. With a little help from some his friends and Havana's City Historian, Papito's barber theme has taken over the whole street, now rechristened 'Hairdressers' Alley' and supported by more than 20 independent businesses.

Plaza del Cristo SQUARE

9 MAP P46, B6

A little apart from the historical core, Plaza del Cristo hasn't benefited from a full restoration yet and this adds subtly to its charm. Here you can sidestep boisterous games of football, listen to the musical outpourings of several cool bars or sit down with half the neighborhood and hook up to the local wi-fi hot spot (in Cuba even the internet is a socially interactive experience!).

Edificio Bacardí LANDMARK

10 MAP P46, B4

Finished in 1930, the magnificent Edificio Bacardí, once the HQ of Cuba's erstwhile rum dynasty, is a triumph of art deco architecture, with a host of lavish finishes utilizing red granite, green marble, terra-cotta reliefs and glazed tiles. Though 12 stories high, it's hemmed in by other buildings these days, so it's hard to get a panoramic view of the structure from street level. Notwithstanding, the opulent bell tower can be glimpsed from all over Havana.

Iglesia y Convento de Nuestra Señora de la Merced CHURCH

11 MAP P46, D7

Bizarrely overlooked by the tourist hordes, this baroque church in its own small square has Havana's most sumptuous ecclesiastical interior, only partially restored. Beautiful gilded altars, frescoed vaults and a number of valuable old paintings create a sacrosanct mood. There's a quiet cloister adjacent.

Iglesia Parroquial del Espíritu Santo CHURCH

12 MAP P46, D7

Havana's oldest surviving church has been remodeled since its founding as a hermitage, built by freed formerly enslaved black people in 1638. Most of the current edifice dates from the mid-19th century and has Moorish, Gothic, neoclassical and Andaluz styles.

Eating

Restaurante Antojos INTERNATIONAL $$

13 MAP P46, B3

A place to satisfy your whims (antojos) if you're whimsical about daiquiris, generously stuffed pulled-pork baguettes or chunky tostones (fried plantain). Wander into the dessert realm (they serve 'em any time) and you'll be equally stirred, particularly if you choose a warm bowl of cinnamon-laced arroz con leche (rice pudding). (☎ 5-277-2577)

El Rum Rum de la Habana

SEAFOOD $$

14 🍴 MAP P46, C3

Not every restaurant has a wine sommelier *and* a cigar sommelier, but this is Havana, and El Rum Rum (the name references both the drink and Cuban slang for 'gossip') can put you straight on every area of consumption courtesy of enthusiastic owner, Osiris Oliver. Everything is outstanding here, from the delicate seafood to the concert-worthy musical entertainment. (elrumrum. restaurantwebexperts.com)

Yarini

CUBAN $$

15 🍴 MAP P46, D8

Located in the emerging street-art district of San Isidro and marked only by a bright neon hat, this rooftop bar/restaurant is named for a once-notorious Havana pimp. Artistic people congregate here to eat, party and parade the latest in T-shirt art on a terrace filled with ferns, foliage and a grandly stacked bar. An exhaustive cocktail menu is backed by adventurous Cuban-influenced food. (yarinihabana.com)

Doña Eutimia

CUBAN $$

16 🍴 MAP P46, D4

The secret at Doña Eutimia is that there *is* no secret: just decent-size portions of the best Cuban food. Expect the likes of *ropa vieja* (shredded beef; there's also an interesting lamb version), epic *picadillo a la habanera* (spicy beef), glorious *lechón asado* (roast pork) and rustic roast

chicken, all served with rice, beans and fried plantains. (📞7-861-1332)

Paladar Los Mercaderes

CUBAN $$$

17 🍴 MAP P46, E5

This restaurant in a historic building has to be one of Cuba's most refined *paladares* (privately run restaurants) for ambience, service and food, both Cuban and international. Follow a marble staircase to a 1st-floor dining room where violinists play and the menu lists the provenance of the farm-to-table food: Cojímar sardines, Pinar del Río pork and Camagüeyan *ropa vieja*. (📞7-861-2437)

D'Next

DINER $

18 🍴 MAP P46, B6

The place to go for well-loaded sandwiches, fruity milkshakes (the *fruta bomba* is outstanding), and late-night coffee and cake cravings. D'Next is a diner-style cafe with air-conditioning, fast service and pop videos on rotation. It remains one of Havana's most reliable places to get decent food without a long wait. Lap it up! (dnext-havana.com/en)

Lo de Monik

TAPAS $$

19 🍴 MAP P46, B3

Eschewing colonial splendor for a French bistro feel, the Monk blends into the chic Loma del Ángel quarter, with a bright-white interior and arguably the city's friendliest staff. Search the blackboard menu for brunch or tapas ideas (fish tacos, well-stuffed Cuban baguettes, cheesecake) and come back later for cocktails. (📞7-864-4029)

5 Sentidos INTERNATIONAL $$

20 🍴 MAP P46, C4

The romantically named five feelings (5 *sentidos*) ought to excite at least three of yours. The open kitchen allows for the free circulation of aromas, the French-bistro decor (painted wood and chandeliers) is pleasing, and your taste buds won't leave unstimulated after you've savored the ceviche, octopus or lamb stew. (📞7-864 8699)

Trattoria 5esquinas ITALIAN $$

21 🍴 MAP P46, C3

Best Italian restaurant in Habana Vieja? There are a few contenders, but 5 esquinas makes a strong claim. It has the full trattoria vibe, right down to the glow of the pizza oven. Italians won't be disappointed with the seafood pasta (generous on the lobster) or the crab-and-spinach cannelloni. Round off your meal with tiramisu. (📞7-860-6295)

Donde Lis CUBAN $$

22 🍴 MAP P46, C4

The Lis' interior is like a love letter to Havana: iconography from the Rat Pack era of the '50s, reproduced 20th-century tropical art, and bright colors splashed onto colonial walls. The menu is a cultivated mélange of flavors, presenting Cuban staples with modern twists – octopus with guacamole, lobster *enchilados* – along with some Italian and Spanish cameos. (dondelis.com)

Paladar Los Mercaderes

Habana 61

CUBAN $$$

23 MAP P46, C3

Habana 61's menu features Cuban classics with a fresh twist. The lobster is among its most popular dishes, but the traditional *ropa vieja* is just as delicious. For a starter, don't miss the cold tomato soup with shrimp. Located in the Loma del Ángel quarter, the small restaurant can fill up quickly. Book ahead. (7-801-6433)

Café Bohemia

TAPAS $

24 MAP P46, D6

Inhabiting a mansion on Plaza Vieja, Café Bohemia – named for a Cuban culture and arts magazine – manages to feel appropriately bohemian but also serves great cocktails, tapas and very addictive cakes. (havanabohemia.com;)

Jíbaro

CUBAN $$

25 MAP P46, E7

Located in a restored colonial mansion in Old Havana's oldest quarter, Jíbaro is a great option for authentic Cuban food and mocktails (nonalcoholic cocktails). Local dishes take a modern twist without getting too gourmet. Stick to the basics and ask for stuffed *tostones, ropa vieja* and black-bean cream. ()

Pistacchio Havana

ICE CREAM $

26 MAP P46, B5

Yet another reason to park yourself in ever-buoyant Plaza del Cristo, this ice-cream parlor with a mezzanine seating area has leapfrogged several of its competitors to wrestle for the prize of best ice cream in Habana Vieja. The tubs lovingly displayed in 16 revolving flavors look like they've been teleported from Italy and the coffee's not bad either.

El Antonia

CUBAN $$

27 MAP P46, B4

Offering *sabor* (taste) and *sonido* (sound) in the heart of Habana Vieja, El Antonia excels in flavorful, well-seasoned food (the *ropa vieja* could well be Havana's best) and suave live music (trova, jazz and *boleros* (ballads) dominate). There's an entryway bar, small stage and interesting decor including wall-mounted chairs, old wardrobes and religious iconography. Come for the evening concerts (and stay for dinner!).

Oasis Nelva

BREAKFAST $

28 MAP P46, C6

Havana's experts on sweet and savory crepes have built a strong reputation on simple foundations. There's an eco-minded recycling aesthetic (jam jars for drinking glasses, old packing cases and tires for stools), along with cheap but generous cocktails, vegetarian options and hearty breakfasts. ()

Buena Vista Curry Club

INDIAN $$

29 MAP P46, C3

Aiming to lure in spice-starved tourists (especially curry-loving

The San Isidro Art District

Bereft of the historical monuments common in other parts of Habana Vieja, the populous San Isidro quarter was largely ignored by outsiders – until the mid-2010s. Before the revolution it was a well-known den of iniquity harboring gamblers and contraband goods; then, from the 1960s onward, it became a tightly packed grid of decaying social housing. The turnaround came in 2016, when the founding of a community art project in collaboration with the Office of the City Historian set the formerly drab streets alight with vivid murals and envelope-pushing art galleries.

One of the main players in the neighborhood's revival is **Galería-Taller Gorría** (Map p46, C8; galeriatallergorria.com), founded by Cuban actor and artist Jorge Perugorría (who starred in the film *Fresa y Chocolate* and the TV miniseries *Cuatro estaciones en La Habana*), on the site of a former bakery.

With the help of several US-based artists, the Gorría gallery has overseen the development of San Isidro's cultural traditions into evocative murals depicting everything from masked faces to abstract animals and birds.

Roughly demarcated by the grid of streets south of Calle Acosta, including Merced, San Isidro and Picota, the neighborhood garnered headlines after the formation of the Movimiento San Isidro in 2018, a body founded to fight censorship. Members of the group have been involved in protests, social media campaigns and hunger strikes.

Brits) and educate Cuban palates in the nuances of Indian food, the Buena Vista Curry Club is a brave venture in a country unaccustomed to fiery *phals* and spicy paneers. (buenavistacurryclub.com; 🖋)

Drinking

El Dandy
CAFE

30 🚍 MAP P46, B6

More stylish man-about-town than vain popinjay, El Dandy is a cafe by day and a cocktail bar by night. A casual greeter shakes your hand at the door, efficient waitstaff take your order at the bar, and trendier-than-you customers pose like peacocks around the marble tables. (bareldandy.com)

Azúcar Lounge
LOUNGE

31 🚍 MAP P46, E6

From a 2nd-floor balcony, high above the architectural beauty contest that is Plaza Vieja, there's no better place in Cuba to savor a piña colada. With its lounge-y seating, trance-y music and avant-garde decor, this is a trendy

Best Breakfasts 🍽️

o **El Café** (Map p46, B5; 🖊️) Tight service, exceptional coffee and homemade sourdough sandwiches supplemented by all-day brunchy breakfasts. This place is rightly popular with indie travelers courtesy of its ample vegan and vegetarian options.

o **La Vitrola** (Map p46, D6) A retro '50s nook on the corner of Plaza Vieja, La Vitrola offers quiet alfresco breakfasts of fruit, coffee, toast and generous omelets, which come complete with a toothpick flag of your home country.

o **Café del Ángel Jacqueline Fumero** (Map p46, B3; cafedelangeljf.com/new-index) Guarding the small, heavenly square behind the Iglesia del Santo Ángel Custodio, minimalist Fumero's mega-popular outdoor tables are excellent perches for egg-based breakfasts and intimate dissections of Havana street life.

place to hang out, but it never feels exclusive. Tourists, premillennials and self-confessed squares will all feel welcome. (📞7-860-6563)

Color Café   CAFE

32 📍 MAP P46, C3

Adding a new shade to Calle Aguiar, this small, perfectly attired cafe-cum-bar-cum-fashion boutique has established a loyal fanbase for its

breakfasts (including waffles), coffee and fun musical vibes that often spill out onto the street. After your libations, take time to peruse the clothes collection on the mezzanine floor. (colorcafehabana.wordpress.com)

Ley Seca   BAR

33 📍 MAP P46, C5

There's long been a clandestine speakeasy atmosphere to Havana so why not milk the idea and open a speakeasy-themed bar? Welcome to Ley Seca (Dry Law) where the booze is above board, jazz drifts out of a low-lit interior, and waitstaff look like they've just walked off the set of an episode of *Peaky Blinders*. Good bruschetta too!

El Floridita   BAR

34 📍 MAP P46, B5

El Floridita was a favorite of expat Americans long before Hemingway dropped by in the '30s, hence the name ('Little Florida'). Bartender Constante Ribalaigua invented the daiquiri here soon after WWI, but it was Hemingway who popularized it and ultimately the bar christened a drink in his honor: the Papa Hemingway Special (a grapefruit-flavored daiquiri). (barfloridita.com)

La Bodeguita del Medio   BAR

35 📍 MAP P46, D4

Made famous thanks to the rum-swilling exploits of Hemingway (who by association instantly sends prices soaring), this is Havana's most celebrated bar. A visit has become de rigueur for tourists who haven't yet cottoned on to the fact that the mojitos are better and (far) cheaper elsewhere.

La Factoria Plaza Vieja BAR

36 MAP P46, D6

Havana's original microbrewery occupies a corner of Plaza Vieja and sells smooth, cold, homemade beer at sturdy wooden benches set up outside on the paving or in a bright, noisy beer hall. Gather a group and you'll get one of three beer varieties (light, amber or dark) in a tall plastic tube with a tap at the bottom.

Café el Escorial CAFE

Once the only cafe on Plaza Vieja, this state-run staple encased in a finely restored colonial mansion, close to Azúcar Lounge (see 31 Map p46, E6) has since been outclassed by private competition. Granted, the caffeine infusions are still pretty good, and it roasts and grinds its own coffee on-site, but the cakes can be as dry as the service.

Museo del Chocolate CAFE

37 MAP P46, E5

Chocolate addicts, beware: this state-run museum-cafe in Habana Vieja's heart is a lethal dose of chocolate, truffles and yet more chocolate (all made on-site). Situated – with no irony intended – on Calle Amargura (literally, Bitterness St), it's more a cafe than a museum. Skip the interior and order your drink from a walk-up window outside next to a churros cart.

Entertainment

Basílica Menor de San Francisco de Asís CLASSICAL MUSIC

38 MAP P46, E5

Plaza de San Francisco de Asís' glorious church, which dates from 1738, has been reincarnated as a 21st-century museum and concert hall. The old nave hosts choral and chamber music on Saturday evenings (check the schedule at the door) and the acoustics are famously good. It's best to bag your ticket at least a day ahead.

Gimnasio de Boxeo Rafael Trejo SPECTATOR SPORT

39 MAP P46, E8

Boxing is hugely popular in Cuba and the country has a long list of Olympic gold medals. Enthusiasts should check out this gym, where you can see fights on Friday at 7pm, or drop by any day after 4pm to watch the training (or even train yourself). (7-862-0266)

Shopping

Clandestina CLOTHING

40 MAP P46, B6

Cuba's first indie design store when it opened in 2015, Clandestina makes T-shirts, bags and accessories out of any materials it can find, 99% of it Cuban. It's the coolest thing around town right now, but it's also eco-conscious and deft at working in a tough economic climate. (clandestina.co)

Habana Vieja Entertainment

Mayuri Tienda Artesanias
GIFTS & SOUVENIRS

41 MAP P46, C4

Curated like a museum, this attractive shop specializes in Panama hats, *guayaberas* (men's shirts) and fine art, but also offers a collection of cigars, wine and rum. The staff are experts in the field and can explain the nuances of the best Cohibas and the finest Havana Club rum. There's another branch in the Loma del Ángel quarter on Calle Chacón 204.

Piscolabis Bazar & Café
HOMEWARES

42 MAP P46, D4

Perfectly located just steps from Havana's 18th-century cathedral (p38), this small but beautifully curated shop is run by a group of Cuban artists of various disciplines and features a wide range of decorative and functional items for the home, as well as jewelry and some clothing. The designers make modern creations from iconic objects of Cuba's past. (piscolabishabana.com)

Librería Venecia
BOOKS

43 MAP P46, B5

Wonderful little private bookshop in Calle Obispo selling yellowed secondhand tomes, esoteric film posters and other random print work that you won't find anywhere else in Havana. A copy of the 2000 edition of the Lonely Planet *Cuba* guidebook was spotted at last visit!

Real Fábrica de Tabacos Partagás Store
CIGARS

44 MAP P46, B5

A prestigious shop affiliated with Havana's main cigar factory (p79) that's housed on a street corner opposite the Parque Francisco de Albear. Not surprisingly, it sells some of Havana's best smokes, including the deep, earthy Partagás brand. Expert cigar aficionados are on hand to enlighten you.

Matty Habana
ARTS & CRAFTS

45 MAP P46, D4

A delightful private shop in a prime spot on Calle Obispo that sells a collection of gift and souvenir-worthy items that contrast with the usual Che Guevara, rum and cigar motifs. You can browse through colorful canvas bags, artisanal lampshades, cute cushions, jewelry, soaps and arty photos, all produced locally.

Centro Cultural Antiguos Almacenes de Deposito San José
ARTS & CRAFTS

46 MAP P46, E8

Havana's multifarious handicraft market sits under the cover of an old shipping warehouse in Desamparados. Check your socialist ideals at the door: herein lies a hive of free enterprise and (unusually for Cuba) haggling. Possible souvenirs include paintings, *guayaberas*, woodwork, leather items, jewelry and numerous apparitions of the highly marketable El Che.

Casa del Habano – Hostal Conde de Villanueva
CIGARS

47 MAP P46, D5

One of Havana's best cigar shops, with its own roller, smoking room and expert sales staff. It's on the mezzanine floor inside a historic tobacco-themed hotel in Calle Mercaderes.

Secondhand Book Market
BOOKS

48 MAP P46, E4

Relocated from Plaza de Armas several years ago, much to the chagrin of many vendors, Havana's famous secondhand-book market convenes in the open-air ruins of the former Casa de Jústiz y Santa Ana. It's an eclectic mix of stallholders selling copies of works by Fidel Castro, Che Guevara and Ernest Hemingway.

Casa Obbatalá
ARTS & CRAFTS

49 MAP P46, B6

This specialist religious shop in Habana Vieja sells all manner of Santería offerings and cult objects, almost exclusively to locals. The costumes, dresses and dolls come in a maelstrom of colors for the different *orishas* (deities) – yellow for Oshún, purple for Babalú Ayé, red for Changó and white for Obbatalá.

La Marca
BODY ART

50 MAP P46, E4

Should you want a memento of your time in Cuba, try La Marca, which was the first licensed tattoo

O'Reilly's Culinary Twins

Fill a small bar restaurant nightly with a buoyant crowd all happy to be enjoying potent cocktails, delectable fish tacos and ceviche, and Havana's tastiest plantain chips, and you've got a guaranteed recipe for success. Indeed, so accomplished was O'Reilly 304 (p43) when it opened in the early 2010s that its owners were soon forced to inaugurate another restaurant directly across the street which they amusingly called El del Frente (p43), meaning 'the one in front.' The newer digs exhibit more of the same culinary genius, with a few bonuses – a roof terrace, retro 1950s design features and heady gin cocktails.

shop on the island. The parlor is run by a group of young Cuban artists who maintain an international level of hygiene, and they sometimes host exhibitions by some of Cuba's leading artists. (lamarcabodyart.com)

Factoria Diseño
DESIGN

51 MAP P46, E6

Gallery/shop showcasing the latest in cutting-edge Cuban art and design, much of it for sale. The large whitewashed room has a neat minimalist layout with objects ranging from jewelry to furniture. There's a cool cafe in which to ponder your transactions.

Top Experience 📷
Climb to the Parque Histórico Militar Morro-Cabaña

Making up arguably the most formidable defensive complex in Spain's erstwhile colonial empire, this unmissable military park, included in the Habana Vieja Unesco World Heritage site, comprises two strapping forts: El Morro, with its emblematic lighthouse, and La Cabaña, a sprawling military bastion famed for its sunset-over-the-Malecón views and theatrical cannon-firing ceremony.

Castillo de los Tres Santos Reyes Magnos del Morro

Perched high on a rocky bluff above the Atlantic, El Morro – the older and smaller of the two forts – was erected between 1589 and 1630 to protect the entrance to Havana harbor from pirates and foreign invaders (French corsair Jacques de Sores had sacked the city in 1555). The fort's irregular polygonal shape, 3m-thick walls and deep protective moat offer a classic example of Renaissance military architecture.

For more than a century the fort withstood numerous attacks by French, Dutch and English privateers, but in 1762, after a 44-day siege, a 12,000-strong British force captured El Morro by attacking from the landward side.

The Castillo's famous **lighthouse** was added in 1844.

Fortaleza de San Carlos de la Cabaña

The impressively hulking La Cabaña (pictured) was built between 1763 and 1774 on a long, exposed ridge on the east side of Havana harbor to fill a weakness in the city's defenses. In 1762 the British had taken Havana by gaining control of this strategically important ridge, and it was from here that they shelled the city mercilessly into submission. In order to prevent a repeat performance, Spanish king Carlos III ordered the construction of a massive fort that would repel future invaders.

Measuring 700m from end to end and covering a whopping 10 hectares, this 18th-century colossus is the largest Spanish colonial fortress in the Americas. The impregnability of the fort meant that no invader ever stormed it, though during the 19th century Cuban patriots faced firing squads here. Dictators Gerardo Machado and Fulgencio Batista used the fortress as a military prison, and immediately after the

★ Top Tip

Hire a horse and cart to ride you into the fort at night. It really adds to the evocative back-to-the-18th-century experience.

✕ Take a Break

There are a couple of bar-restaurants inside La Cabaña fort or the privately run **Paladar Doña Carmela** (☎ 7-867-7472) just outside.

★ Getting There

🚌 Take metro bus P-15 from Centro Habana.

🚕 A taxi from Habana Vieja should cost around US$5.

⛴ The Casablanca ferry departs from Emboque de Luz in Habana Vieja.

revolution Che Guevara set up his headquarters inside the ramparts to preside over another catalog of grisly executions (this time of Batista's officers).

These days the fort has been restored for visitors, and you can spend at least half a day checking out its wealth of attractions, including museums, bars, restaurants, souvenir stalls and a cigar shop (containing the world's longest cigar).

Museo de Comandancia del Che

The Museo de Comandancia del Che is probably the most interesting of the several museums spread around Havana's two eastern forts. It's a diminutive but nonetheless riveting exposé on the life and

times of Ernesto Guevara de la Serna ('El Che'), and inhabits his old office in La Cabaña fort, from where he meted out revolutionary 'justice' in 1959. The story of his life is told with pictures and a few belongings (radios, rucksacks and guns).

Museo de Fortificaciones y Armas

Inside the Fortaleza de San Carlos de la Cabaña, this armaments museum contains weapons from bows and arrows to giant catapults and cannons.

Cañonazo Ceremony

Every night at 9pm, actors dressed in full 18th-century military regalia reenact the firing of a cannon over

The British Siege of El Morro

Spanish military strategists had warned for years that the high ridge now occupied by La Cabaña fort was a point of vulnerability. Their words were prophetic. In 1762, during the so-called Seven Years' War, the British occupied the then undefended ridge without losing a man and used that position to shell both El Morro fort and the city of Havana across the harbor. The siege lasted 44 days before the Spanish surrendered. Humiliated by their loss, they resolved not to repeat their mistake and, on regaining Havana in exchange for Florida in 1763, they buttressed the ridge with a truly massive defensive structure, La Cabaña.

the harbor in La Cabaña fort. In days of yore the shot marked the closing of the old city gates. With its solemn marching and the lights of Havana twinkling in the background, it's still a highly atmospheric ceremony.

Salas & Exhibits

Exhibits inside El Morro provide essential background on both forts within the military park, plus a perfect scale model of El Morro itself. There's also a room profiling the successful British attack on the fort in 1762, an episode that provoked the Spanish to build La Cabaña a decade later. The story is told through a series of painted canvases depicting the events of the battle, and is complemented by written commentaries in English and Spanish.

Nearby: Estatua de Cristo

This impossible-to-miss statue on a rise on the harbor's eastern side was created by Jilma Madera in 1958. It was promised to President Batista by his wife after the US-backed leader survived an attempt on his life in the Presidential Palace in March 1957, and was (ironically) unveiled on Christmas Day 1958, one week before the dictator fled the country. As you disembark the Casablanca ferry, follow the road uphill for about 10 minutes until you reach the monument.

The views from up here are stupendous and it's a favorite nighttime hangout for the local youth.

Top Experience 📷

Uncover Santería at the Iglesia de Nuestra Señora de Regla

As important as it is diminutive, this modest church on the eastern shores of Havana harbor shelters the blessed virgin of Regla worshipped by Catholics and adherents of Santería (who call her Yemayá) with equal fervor. The virgin's statue was brought to Havana in the 1690s and harks back to a devotional cult that originated in Spain in the 5th century.

The Church

The settlement of Regla grew up around a shrine first built here in 1687. The church went through various incarnations until the current structure was erected in 1810, by which time the virgin had been declared the patron saint of the port of Havana. The chapel-like building with its blue wooden doors and heavy ceiling beams is colonial in style. Inside, alcoves reveal statues of the saints and a gold-leaf altar is dominated by a depiction of the black virgin in her customary blue robes.

The Venerated Virgin

The virgin, represented by a black Madonna, is venerated in the Catholic faith and associated in the Santería religion with Yemayá, the *orisha* (deity) of the ocean and the patron of sailors (always represented in blue). Legend claims that this image was carved by St Augustine 'The African' in the 5th century, and that in 453 CE a disciple brought the statue to Spain to safeguard it from barbarians. The small vessel in which the image was traveling survived a storm in the Strait of Gibraltar, so the figure was recognized as the patron of sailors. In more recent times, Cuban rafters attempting to reach the US have also evoked the protection of the Black Virgin.

The Vendors

It is rare to find the church empty. Pilgrims regularly file in to pray quietly and offer gifts to the virgin. A semipermanent posse of vendors awaits outside the church selling flowers, trinkets and Santería dolls. Some of them lay out tarot cards and offer to tell fortunes.

★ Top Tips

o For full Regla immersion, visit on September 7, the virgin's feast day, when the statue is taken from the church and paraded around the neighborhood.

o To broaden your knowledge of Santería stroll up to the **Museo Municipal de Regla** after visiting the church.

✕ Take a Break

o There is very little in the way of good restaurants in Regla.

o **Bar Dos Hermanos** near the Emboque de Luz ferry dock (on the Habana Vieja side of the harbor) is a good place to wet your whistle before jumping on a boat.

★ Getting There

⛴ Regla is easily accessible on the passenger ferry that departs every 20 minutes from the Emboque de Luz at the intersection of Av del Puerto and Santa Clara in Habana Vieja.

Explore ⊗
Centro Habana

Centro Habana's crowded residential grid offers an uncensored look at Cuba without the fancy wrapping paper. On its potholed but perennially action-packed streets, elderly men engage in marathon games of dominoes, Afro-Cuban drums beat out addictive rumba rhythms and mildewed down-at-heel buildings give intriguing hints of their illustrious previous lives.

The Short List

○ **Museo Nacional de Bellas Artes (p68)** Viewing the full encyclopedia of Cuban art at this wonderful two-campus museum.

○ **Capitolio Nacional (p70)** Visiting Cuba's exquisitely restored legislature building with its soaring dome, Grecian columns and palatial interior.

○ **Centro Habana Streetlife (p72)** Uncovering the richness that lives within the dense urban streets of this superficially shabby neighborhood.

○ **Malecón (p73)** Dodging waves and cars on Havana's magnificent sea drive.

○ **Callejón de Hamel (p76)** Getting into the rhythm of the rumba drummers in this multicolored back alley.

Getting There & Around

🚌 Parque de la Fraternidad is Centro Habana's main transport nexus, with metro buses and the Havana Tour Bus fanning out all over the city.

🚗 Taxis galore congregate in Parque Central. For cheaper fares in Cuban *almendrones* (shared taxis), head to Parque El Curita at the corner of Dragones and Aguila.

Centro Habana Map on p74

Top Experience 📷

See Cuban Painting at the Museo Nacional de Bellas Artes

Spread over two campuses, the Bellas Artes is arguably the finest art gallery in the Caribbean. The 'Arte Cubano' building contains the most comprehensive collection of Cuban art in the world, while the 'Arte Universal' section is laid out in a grand eclectic palace overlooking Parque Central, with exterior flourishes that are just as impressive as the art within.

◉ MAP P74, G3

bellasartes.co.cu

Arte Cubano Collection

The Cuban collection is exhibited in the original **museum building** on Trocadero, between Agramonte and Av de las Misiones, which dates from 1955. Works are displayed in chronological order, starting on the 3rd floor, and are surprisingly varied. Artists to look out for include Guillermo Collazo, considered to be the first truly great Cuban artist; Rafael Blanco, with his cartoon-like paintings and sketches; Raúl Martínez, a master of 1960s Cuban pop art; and the Picasso-like Wifredo Lam.

Arte Universal Collection

Since 2001 the international collection, displaying art from 500 BCE to the present day, has been exhibited on three floors of the **Palacio de los Asturianos**, located on San Rafael between Agramonte and Av de las Misiones. Its undisputed highlight is its Spanish collection, with canvases by Francisco de Zurbarán, Bartolomé Esteban Murillo and Jusepe de Ribera, and a tiny work by Diego Velázquez. Also worth perusing are the 2000-year-old Roman mosaics, Greek pots from the 5th century BCE, and a suitably refined canvas by Thomas Gainsborough (in the British room).

La Gitana Tropical

Sometimes dubbed the 'Mona Lisa of the Caribbean,' this simple but haunting study of a woman by Havana-born painter Víctor Manuel García Valdés was executed in Paris in 1929 and shows distinct European influences. Valdés was part of the Vanguardia movement of artists and his *Gitana* isn't just the country's most cherished painting but also serves as a precursor to Cuban modernism.

★ Top Tips

o If you're short on time, admire the Centro Asturianos from the outside and the more topical (and tropical) Arte Cubano collection from within.

o Buying a joint ticket for admission to both galleries will save you time and money.

o There's a lot to see. Set aside a good 90 minutes for each museum.

✖ Take a Break

Both museums have cafes, but they're better for drinks than for food. **Cafe Baco** in the Arte Universal building is fabulously decorated with Sevillan *azulejos* (tiles).

It's not at all sloppy and Joe no longer works there, but Sloppy Joe's (p84), midway between the two museums, does a mean spicy-beef sandwich.

Top Experience 📷

Be Dazzled by Gold and Marble at the Capitolio Nacional

The incomparable Capitolio Nacional is Havana's most ambitious and grandiose building, constructed after the post-WWI boom ('Dance of the Millions') gifted the Cuban government a seemingly bottomless vault of sugar money. Until 1959 it was the seat of the Cuban Congress and in 2019 it reopened after six years of refurbishments to serve once again as Cuba's National Assembly.

◎ MAP P74, G4

Construction & Refurbishment

Similar to the Capitol building in Washington, DC, but actually modeled on the Panthéon in Paris, the building was initiated by Cuba's US-backed dictator Gerardo Machado in 1926 and took 5000 workers three years, two months and 20 days to construct, at a cost of US$17 million.

Formerly the Capitolio was the seat of the Cuban Congress, then from 1959 to 2013 it housed the Cuban Academy of Sciences and the National Library of Science and Technology. From 2013 the building underwent a six-year refurbishment, reopening in time for Havana's 500th anniversary as Cuba's National Assembly.

Salón de los Pasos Perdidos

The entryway is accessed by a sweeping 55-step staircase guarded by two giant statues carved by Italian sculptor Angelo Zanelli: *El Trabajo* (male) and *La Virtud Tutelar* (female). The main doors open into the Salón de los Pasos Perdidos (Room of the Lost Steps; pictured), so named because of its unusual acoustics. At its centerpoint, directly under the cupola, stands a magnificent statue of *La República,* an enormous bronze woman standing 17.6m tall and symbolizing the mythic Guardian of Virtue and Work. The 30-tonne statue is covered in gold leaf and is the third-largest indoor statue in the world. It was carved by Zanelli in Rome and shipped to Cuba in three pieces.

Other Rooms

Two legislative chambers lie at either end of the building: the chamber of representatives and the chamber of deputies (the Senate). Guided tours visit the former. You will also be able to peep into sumptuous governmental offices furnished in exuberant French rococo and Empire styles.

★ Top Tips

o Admission is by guided tour only. Buy tickets at the Arton bookshop opposite.

o Tours last 45 minutes and leave on the hour.

o Tours take in most of the building's main features, including the grand hallways, the chamber of representatives and various opulently decorated offices.

o Don't miss the former committee rooms containing original casts of Zanelli's statues plus a collection of state china. Also viewable are two inner courtyards that help control temperatures in the building and add welcome splashes of green.

✕ Take a Break

There is currently no refreshment inside the Capitolio, but there are plenty of options nearby, including Siá Kará Café (p83), five minutes' walk away, which serves food, cocktails and coffee.

Walking Tour 🥾

Centro Habana Streetlife

Life in Centro Habana goes on irrespective of tourism, inclement weather or the distractions of the internet age. During the day this ebullient but dilapidated neighborhood is a microcosm of Cuban life – it's the city's most densely populated district, with 135,000 people squeezed into a 3-sq-km grid. At night it resembles a shady, old-fashioned movie set.

Walk Facts

Start cnr Prado and Trocadero

End Cayo Hueso

Length 3.5km; 1½ hours

❶ El Prado

On weekends the tree-shaded European-style walkway that cuts down the center of El Prado is filled with Cuban artists producing, displaying and selling their work. The rest of the week you can practice your sidestepping skills with soccer-playing kids and schoolteachers holding physical education classes.

❷ Esquina Caliente

Follow the shouts emanating from the omnipresent group of men who stand arguing near the José Martí statue in Parque Central (p78). The topic is generally baseball and the melee is known as the *esquina caliente* ('hot corner'), after the corner of Calles 23 and 12 in Vedado where it originally convened.

❸ El Bulevar

The pedestrianized section of Calle San Rafael near the Hotel Inglaterra, known to *habaneros* as El Bulevar, is an unashamedly local affair, with peso snack stalls, half-bare grocery shops and 1950s shopping nostalgia.

❹ Parque de la Fraternidad

Want a picture of one of those old American cars? Dozens of *almendrones* wait around the Capitolio in what has been dubbed Jurassic Park. The park's real name, Parque de la Fraternidad, is meant to signify brotherhood with the Americas, hence the busts of American leaders.

❺ El Barrio Chino

Havana's El Barrio Chino is notable for its lack of Chinese residents. However, in the 1990s the Cuban government recognized the area's tourist potential and sought to rejuvenate its historical character.

❻ Calle Galiano

The street officially called Av de Italia is still referred to by *habaneros* as Calle Galiano. Serving as Centro Habana's main drag, it was once lined with plush department stores. These days the demeanor is more downbeat, although the action is just as lively.

❼ Malecón

Glimpse the uncensored Cuba on Havana's 7km-long Malecón sea drive, where hundreds of *habaneros* come to stroll at sunset.

❽ Cayo Hueso

The cauldron full of old sticks is a *nganga* (Palo Monte altar) and the people dressed in white are *Iyabós* (Santería initiates). Welcome to Cayo Hueso, a subdistrict of Centro Habana with a strong Afro-Cuban heritage. The area is centered on the Callejón de Hamel (p76), a paint-spattered alley rightly famous for its Sunday rumba drummers.

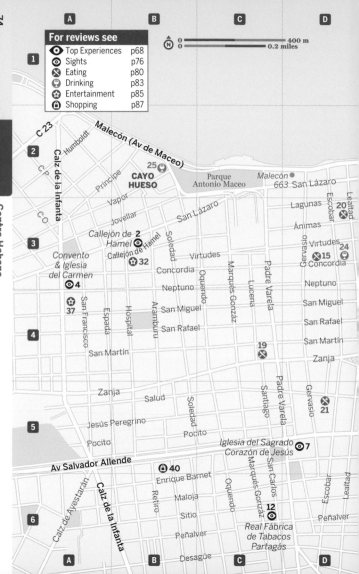

A **B** **C** **D**

For reviews see
- ◉ Top Experiences p68
- ◉ Sights p76
- ⊗ Eating p80
- ☕ Drinking p83
- ★ Entertainment p85
- ⬤ Shopping p87

0 ——————— 400 m
0 ——————— 0.2 miles

Malecón (Av de Maceo)

C 23

Humboldt

Calz de la Infanta

C P

C O

Príncipe

CAYO HUESO

25

Parque Antonio Maceo

Malecón 663 San Lázaro

Vapor

San Lázaro

Lagunas

Escobar

Leatlad

20

Jovellar

Ánimas

Gervasio

Virtudes 24

Callejón de 2 Hamel ◉

Soledad

Virtudes

⊗15 ⬤

Convento & Iglesia del Carmen ◉4

Callejón de Hamel

★32

Concordia

Oquendo

Marqués González

Lucena

Padre Varela

Concordia

Neptuno

Neptuno

San Miguel

★37

San Francisco

Espada

Hospital

Aramburu

San Miguel

San Rafael

San Rafael

San Martín

San Martín

Zanja

19

⊗

Zanja

Santiago

Padre Varela

Gervasio

Salud

Soledad

Jesús Peregrino

Pocito

Pocito

Iglesia del Sagrado Corazón de Jesús ◉7

⊗21

Av Salvador Allende

⬤40

Enrique Barnet

Retiro

Maloja

Oquendo

Marqués González

San Carlos

Escobar

Leatlad

Calz de Ayestarán

Calz de la Infanta

Sitio

Peñalver

12 ◉

Peñalver

Real Fábrica de Tabacos Partagás

Desagüe

A **B** **C** **D**

E F G H

1

Castillo de
San Salvador
de la Punta

Straits of Florida

28

Av. de los Estudiantes

Cárcel
Palacio
Velasco **14**

Tacón

Genios

Agramonte

Malecón

27

San Lázaro

Refugio

Museo de la
Revolución

Aguiar

2

Crespo

Colón

41

Aguila

Consulado

Escuela
Nacional
de Ballet 8

Av. de las Misiones

Chacón

Compostela

Tejadillo

Havana
Super
Tour

18

Trocadero

Paseo de Martí (Prado)

Aguacate

Empedrado

Bernal

Museo Nacional
de Bellas Artes

San Juan de Dios

Ánimas

Palacio de los 6

O'Reilly

3

Av. de Italia (Galiano)

San Nicolás

Virtudes

Matrimonios 31

39 30

Obispo

Campanario

Taller Comunitario
José Martí

Obrapía

Compostela

34

29

3

Neptuno

Lamparilla

33

17

5

10

San
Rafael

San Miguel

Hotel Inglaterra

Parque

Aguacate

4

16

San Rafael

Gran Teatro de la
Habana Alicia Alonso 1

Central

Cristo

Villegas

Av. de Italia (Galiano)

Capitolio
Nacional

Agramonte

Muralla

EL BARRIO
CHINO

Cuchillo

Barcelona

Bernaza

Dragones

23

26

22

Sol

Zanja

38

Salud

Fuente
de la
India

36

Luz

Parque
El Curita

Dragones

Parque de la 11
Fraternidad

13

Asociación Cultural
Yoruba de Cuba

Av. de Bélgica

5

Av Simón Bolívar

Enrique Barnet

Corrales

Acosta

Jesús María

Manrique

San Nicolás

Rayo

Maloja

Factoría

Suárez

Cárdenas

Economía

Cienfuegos

35

Merced

Sitio

Apodaca

Aponte

Gloria

Máximo Gómez

Revillagigedo

Misión

Old
City

6

Indio

Aguila

Estación Central
de Ferrocarriles
(Central Train Station)

9

La Coubre
(200m)

E F G H

Sights

Gran Teatro de la Habana Alicia Alonso

THEATER

1 ⊙ MAP P74, G4

The neobaroque Gran Teatro de la Habana Alicia Alonso, erected as a Galician social club between 1907 and 1914, features highly ornate and even exuberant architectural details. It's the official stage for the Cuban National Ballet Company and the headquarters of the biennial **International Ballet Festival**. Dance presentations, ranging from ballet to contemporary dance to Spanish-influenced choreography by companies from all over the country and abroad, are the highlights every weekend. There are daily guided tours. (balletcuba. cult.cu)

Callejón de Hamel

STREET

2 ⊙ MAP P74, B3

There are at least four reasons that you should incorporate this community-driven back alley into any serious Havana outing: first, it's the unofficial HQ of Havana's Afro-Cuban community; second, it's replete with inspired street art, much of it executed with recycled materials (this is where your old bathtub gets a new life); third, it's an essential stop for anyone trying to understand Cuba's complex syncretic religions; and, fourth, the denizens put on hypnotic live rumba shows (p85) every Sunday.

Taller Comunitario José Martí

GALLERY

3 ⊙ MAP P74, G3

Workshop-gallery of an avant-garde artists' collective comprising around a dozen artists. Enter via the radiant mural in El Prado to admire and/or buy probing, cutting-edge creations and chat to their makers.

Convento & Iglesia del Carmen

CHURCH

4 ⊙ MAP P74, A3

This little-visited church's bell tower dominates the Centro Habana skyline and is topped by a huge statue of Nuestra Señora del Carmen, but the real prizes are inside: rich Seville-style tiles, a gilded altarpiece, ornate woodcarving and swirling frescoes. Surprisingly, the church was only constructed in 1923, to house a Carmelite order. The building is considered 'eclectic.'

Hotel Inglaterra

HISTORIC BUILDING

5 ⊙ MAP P74, G3

Havana's oldest hotel opened its doors in 1856 on the site of a popular bar called El Louvre (the hotel's alfresco bar still bears that name). Facing leafy Parque Central (p78), the building exhibits the neoclassical design features in vogue at the time, complemented by a lobby beautified with Moorish tiles. At a banquet here in 1879, José Martí made a speech advocating Cuban independence, and much later US journalists covering the Spanish–American

Hotel Inglaterra

War stayed at the hotel.
(hotelinglaterralahabana.com)

Palacio de los Matrimonios

NOTABLE BUILDING

6 ⊙ MAP P74, G3

In largely secular Cuba, this is where many *habaneros* come to get married and – appropriately – the building is no less lavish than a church. Built as a Spanish social club in 1914, the neo-Renaissance palace is ornate inside and out and boasts sweeping staircases and an elaborately frescoed ballroom.

Iglesia del Sagrado Corazón de Jesús

CHURCH

7 ⊙ MAP P74, D5

A little out of the way but well worth the walk is this inspiring marble

creation with a distinctive white steeple – it's one of Cuba's few Gothic buildings. The church is rightly famous for its magnificent stained-glass windows, and the light that penetrates the eaves first thing in the morning (when the church is deserted) gives the place a strange ethereal quality.

Escuela Nacional de Ballet

NOTABLE BUILDING

8 ⊙ MAP P74, G2

The neoclassical Escuela Nacional de Ballet, Alicia Alonso's famous ballet school, overlooks the tree-lined Prado. It's the largest ballet school in the world, with over 3000 students, and also one of the most prestigious. The tickling of ivories and the tapping of dainty feet can often be heard amid the growling of the vintage cars outside.

Old City Wall
HISTORIC SITE

9 MAP P74, H6

In the 17th century, anxious to defend the city from attacks by pirates and overzealous foreign armies, Cuba's paranoid colonial authorities drew up plans for the construction of a 5km-long city wall. Built between 1674 and 1740, the wall on completion was 1.5m thick and 10m high, running along a line now occupied by Av de las Misiones and Av de Bélgica.

Parque Central
PARK

10 MAP P74, G3

Diminutive Parque Central is a verdant haven from the belching buses and roaring taxis that ply the Paseo de Martí. Long a microcosm of daily Havana life, the park was expanded to its present size in the late 19th century after the city walls were knocked down. The 1905 marble **statue of José Martí** at its center was the first of thousands to be erected in Cuba. It's surrounded by 28 palm trees.

Fuente de la India
MONUMENT

11 MAP P74, G5

Spare a glance for this white Carrara-marble fountain, carved by Giuseppe Gaggini in 1837 for the Count of Villanueva and now situated on a traffic island in front of the shell of the Hotel Saratoga. It portrays a regal indigenous woman adorned with a crown of eagle's

Parque Central

The Malecón Sea Drive

Sometimes dubbed 'the world's longest sofa,' the Malecón is a sweeping 7km-long sea drive that stretches from the cusp of Habana Vieja to the fringes of Miramar, incorporating some of the city's most evocative monuments and buildings.

Habaneros of all types congregate here to gossip, party, meditate and masquerade, using the corroded seawall like it's an alfresco extension of their living rooms. There are the amorous first-daters, the street poets, the rum ranters, the Florida-gazers clasping their fishing rods and the talented musicians practicing their arpeggios. The atmosphere intensifies at sunset, when the sky turns a streaky orange, lending the mildewed facades of Centro Habana a distinctly romantic quality.

Neglect and the destructive effects of the ocean have left many of the thoroughfare's buildings facing decrepitude and irrevocable damage. Several new hotels have sought to reverse the slide.

The Malecón is transformed when a cold front blows in and massive waves crash over the sea wall. The road is often closed to cars at these times, meaning you can walk along the middle of the street and get a thorough soaking.

feathers and seated on a throne surrounded by four gargoylesque dolphins.

Real Fábrica de Tabacos Partagás   FACTORY

12 MAP P74, C6

One of Havana's oldest and most famous cigar businesses, the Real Fábrica de Tabacos Partagás was founded in 1845 by Spaniard Jaime Partagás. In 2013 the factory moved from its original location behind the Capitolio (p70) to its current digs just off Calle Padre Varela in Centro Habana. It's the only cigar factory in Havana offering reliable tours. Tickets must be bought beforehand in the lobby of any of the hotels on Parque Central.

Asociación Cultural Yoruba de Cuba   MUSEUM

13 MAP P74, G5

To untangle the mysteries of the Santería religion, its saints and their powers, decamp to this museum–cultural center. Aside from sculpted effigies of the various *orishas* (deities), the association hosts *tambores* (Santería drum ceremonies) on Friday at 6pm. Check the noticeboard at the door for details. Note that there's a church dress code for the *tambores* (no shorts or tank tops).

Havana Super Tour ⤵

A well-established private tour company, **Havana Super Tour** (Map p74, E2; campanario63. com) runs all its trips in classic American cars. The two most popular are the art deco architectural tour and the 'Mob tour,' uncovering the city's pre-revolution Mafia haunts. If you're short on time, the full-blown Havana day tour will whip you around all of the city's key sights.

Palacio Velasco

NOTABLE BUILDING

14 👁 MAP P74, G2

Now the Spanish embassy, this beautiful wedding-cake-like building was constructed in the art nouveau style in 1912. It's the only embassy in this part of town.

Eating

La Guarida

INTERNATIONAL $$$

15 🍴 MAP P74, D3

Only in Havana! The entrance to the city's most legendary private restaurant greets you like a scene out of a 1940s film noir. A decapitated statue lies at the bottom of a grand but dilapidated staircase that leads past lines of drying clothes to a wooden door, beyond which lie multiple culinary surprises. (laguarida.com)

San Cristóbal

CUBAN $$$

16 🍴 MAP P74, E4

San Cristóbal was knocking out fine food long before the US president dropped by in March 2016, although the publicity surrounding Barack Obama's visit probably didn't hurt. Crammed into one of Centro Habana's grubbier streets, the restaurant has a museum-worthy interior crowded with old photos, animal hides and a Santería altar flanked by images of Antonio Maceo and José Martí. (📞7-867-9109)

Real Habana

CUBAN $$

17 🍴 MAP P74, F3

On the cusp of Centro Habana's gritty but unthreatening 'hood (a semi-permanent posse of moneychangers guard the door), this salt-of-the-earth restaurant gets you away from the tourist-ville of Parque Central and into a world of Spanish-only menus, 90% local diners, and *criolla* classics offered at affordable prices. Good steaks too!

Castas y Tal

CUBAN $$

18 🍴 MAP P74, E2

Finding a balance by attracting Cubans (with economical prices and traditional recipes) and tourists (with creative 'fusion' touches), hip C&T is a bistro-style restaurant encased by the Centro Habana 'hood. High-quality, adventurous food, such as lamb with masala or chicken in orange sauce, is backed up with Cuban classics (lashings of rice and beans are served on the side). (📞 7-864-2177)

Barbra Restaurante Bar
INTERNATIONAL $$

19 🍴 MAP P74, C4

Adding a Miami-esque flourish to the time-ravaged streets of Centro Habana, Barbra is a highly ambitious private restaurant that leaves a vivid impression with its polished glasses, formal service and decadent grand piano that anchors a large, glossy interior. The Cuban-Italian food matches the setting, especially if you opt for the peppery beef tenderloin or the extravagant ceviche. (📞 7-878-1699)

Casa Miglis
SWEDISH $$

20 🍴 MAP P74, D3

There are many unusual juxta-positions at this Swedish-Cuban restaurant, hidden inside a battle-scarred tenement, where the cool Scandinavian-style interior is punctuated by the kind of avant-garde art that might have sprung from the mind of Ingmar Bergman. Then there's the food: a smorgas-bord of international delights given extra zest by a couple of Swedish classics. (casamiglis.com)

Mimosa
ITALIAN $$

21 🍴 MAP P74, D5

Locally lauded restaurant in Chinatown that specializes in – guess what – pizza. It's famous for its long lines, huge portions and

San Cristóbal

very Cuban pizza (heavily loaded, *mucho* ham and not much crust). It's also perfected numerous other dishes, including rich desserts and the croquettes you see everywhere these days. Prices are reasonable and there's plenty of loud neighborhood ambience!

Los Nardos
SPANISH $$

22 🍴 MAP P74, G4

Belonging to one of several Spanish aid societies in Havana (in this case the Asturianos), Nardos looks like another distressed Havana tenement from the outside but resembles a dark-wood, dark-lit gentlemen's club within. The Cuban-Spanish food is famously cheap and plentiful and served by speedy, waistcoated staff members. Paella, chicken and pork dishes don't break US$5. Even the lobster's cheap! (📞7-863-2985)

Restaurante Tien-Tan
CHINESE $$

23 🍴 MAP P74, E4

One of the few authentic Chinese restaurants in El Barrio Chino (p73), Tien-Tan (Temple of Heaven) is run by a Chinese-Cuban couple and serves an incredible 130 dishes. Try chop suey with vegetables or chicken with cashews and sit outside in action-packed Cuchillo, a narrow pedestrianized alley replete with cheap restaurants. (📞7-863-2081)

Café Arcángel (p84)

Drinking

Michifú
BAR

24 ⬤ MAP P74, D3

An effortlessly cool piano bar adorned with pop-art lampshades and color-accented sofas. Flop down amid a crash pad of cushions and imbibe rum-laced cocktails as the local musical prodigies practice their Tchaikovsky. The tranquil ambience is an excellent appetizer for dinner at the nearby culinary institutions of La Guarida (p80) or San Cristóbal (p80).

El Bleco
BAR

25 ⬤ MAP P74, B2

Since its 2022 opening, El Bleco has quickly established itself as one of Havana's most fashionable places to sink a cocktail. On the open-roofed sea-view terrace, DJs curate ambient music while waitstaff – most of whom look like off-duty dancers – serve drinks, much-talked-about pizza, and a unique Nutella and focaccia dessert. Trendy but pricey.

Siá Kará Café
BAR

26 ⬤ MAP P74, F4

In Starbucks-free Havana, every cafe is individual and Siá Kará exhibits its character with graffiti-covered tables, an old tie collection and a parody of the *Mona Lisa* flipping the bird. Although ostensibly a bar-cafe, it serves everything from Varadero lobster to crusty

Malecón 663

Even if you're not staying over, it is still well worth checking out this French-Cuban boutique **hotel** (Map p74, D2; malecon663.com) on the Malecón, a whimsical mélange of art, recycling, comfort and sophistication.

Non-guests can enjoy a downstairs cafe crammed with artistic creations based on Cuba's recycling ethic, and a rooftop terrace that mixes fine mojitos after 6pm; the terrace also has a Jacuzzi (for guests only). A very cool concept store on the ground floor, close to the entrance, sells unique locally made fashion accessories.

chicken sandwiches. The cushioned benches under the stairs are the perfect place to crack open a thick novel. (☎7-867-4084)

Blanco 9
BAR

27 ⬤ MAP P74, F2

Sequestered in a short, narrow street just off the Malecón, this diminutive bar is hard to spot in the daytime but impossible to miss on weekend nights, when it hosts packed street parties that pulsate with electronic music. Join the throng amid colored lights, crowd-rousing DJs and dancers on stilts.

The Rise of the Grafiteros

Art in Cuba has always been one of the most effective forms of social commentary. Subtly nuanced works by Cuban artists are often loaded with hidden messages or *dos sentidos* (double meanings) and can deliver a powerful political message. Yet, while heavy-handed censorship has been relaxed since the 1980s, artists must still be careful how they frame their ideas. Large, tourist-attracting street-art projects such as Fusterlandia are generally tolerated; direct attacks on the government are not.

Unauthorized graffiti is a relatively new phenomenon in Havana that would not have been possible 15 years ago. One of the city's most daring and visible new *grafiteros* goes by the moniker 2+2=5. The name itself is subversive, a reference to the slogan in George Orwell's novel *Nineteen Eighty-Four* through which a one-party state legitimized its false dogma. Since 2016, 2+2=5 has used a recurring character, *'supermalo,'* a cartoonish minion masked by a balaclava, to make comments about contemporary culture. *Supermalo* features all over Havana in places such as the emerging San Isidro Art District in Habana Vieja and ruined tenements on the Malecón. He is often joined by work from other *grafiteros,* such as Yulier P, known for his contorted human faces, and Cuban-American Abstrk, whose magnificent *Green Girl* adorns a wall in San Isidro.

Origenes CAFE

28 MAP P74, G1

The best part of Havana's five-star hotel giant on the corner of Prado and the Malecón could well be the narrow waterside Origenes bar, where you can hunker down to coffee and pastries from an artistically designed display case as the waves lash against the seawall. (royaltonresorts.com/resorts/habana)

Café Arcángel CAFE

29 MAP P74, F3

Excellent coffee, fine croissants, suave non-reggaeton music and Charlie Chaplin movies playing on a loop in a scarred Centro Habana apartment – what more could you want? (cafearcangel.com)

Sloppy Joe's BAR

30 MAP P74, G3

Opened by young Spanish immigrant José García (aka 'Joe') in 1919, this bar earned its name for its dodgy sanitation and soggy *ropa vieja* (shredded beef) sandwich. Legendary among expats before the revolution, it closed in the '60s after a fire but was reincarnated in 2013 behind the same noble neoclassical facade. And it's still serving decent cocktails and soggy sandwiches. (📞 7-866-7157)

Plan H   WINE BAR

31 🚇 MAP P74, G3

A first for Cuba, this pioneering enoteca and delicatessen was founded in 2023 by Ada Dimbath, a Cuban who spent many years living in Germany. It has an extensive wine cellar with carefully chosen vintages, from Chilean chardonnays to Spanish cab savs, which you can buy or taste in its elegant little wine bar on El Prado. There's a small on-site deli stocked with ham, cheese and other deluxe groceries. (enotecahabana.com)

Cafe El Louvre   CAFE

The animated sidewalk cafe at the Hotel Inglaterra (see 5 ⊙ Map p74, G3) is an open terrace bar where mojitos and Cuba Libres are served well before noon. It's the perfect place to watch Havana's vibrant Parque Central (p78) to the soundtrack of the live bands that play here daily. (📶)

Entertainment

Callejón de Hamel Live Rumba   LIVE MUSIC

32 🎭 MAP P74, B3

Aside from its funky murals and psychedelic art shops, the main reason to come to this alleyway (p76) is Havana's high temple of

Afro-Cuban culture, is the frenetic rumba music that kicks off every Sunday around noon.

Gran Teatro de la Habana Alicia Alonso   THEATER

Havana's fabulous 'great' theater (see 1 ⊙ Map p74, G4) underwent an extensive refurbishment in the late 2010s and continues to offer up the best in Cuban dance and music. Its specialty is ballet (it's the headquarters of the Cuban National Ballet), but it also stages musicals, plays and opera. Check the noticeboard for upcoming events. (balletcuba.cult.cu)

Casa de la Música   LIVE MUSIC

33 🎭 MAP P74, F3

One of two such establishments in the city, this legendary place is where Cubans and tourists who don't want to be treated like tourists go for full-on *caliente* music and dancing. All the big names play here, from Bamboleo to Los Van Van – and you'll pay peanuts to see them.

Teatro América   THEATER

34 🎭 MAP P74, E3

Housed in a classic art deco *rascacielo* (skyscraper), the América seems to have changed little since its theatrical heyday in the 1930s and '40s. It hosts variety, comedy, dance, jazz and salsa; shows are normally held on Saturday at 8:30pm and on Sunday at 5pm.

El Guajirito
LIVE MUSIC

35 ⭐ MAP P74, H5

Some label it a tourist trap, but this restaurant-entertainment space bivouacked upstairs in a deceptively dilapidated Havana tenement plays some of the most professional Buena Vista Social Club music you'll ever hear. Indeed, this is a Buena Vista Social Club of sorts. (📞7-863-3009)

Sociedad Cultural Rosalia de Castro
LIVE MUSIC

36 ⭐ MAP P74, G5

A slightly cheaper alternative to the nearby Guajirito, this venue puts on nightly shows that don't stray too far from the classic Buena Vista Social Club repertoire. Tickets can be purchased with or without dinner. Skip the food. (📞5-270-5271)

Cine Infanta
CINEMA

37 ⭐ MAP P74, A4

A multiplex cinema that's plush by Cuban standards, Infanta is an important venue during December's **international film festival** (p15).

Teatro Martí
THEATER

38 ⭐ MAP P74, G4

Known also as the 'theater of a hundred doors' (in reference to the French windows adorning its exterior), this neoclassical gem is a masterpiece of restoration. After 40 years in dereliction, it reopened in 2014 with new air-conditioning and audio equipment, an orchestra pit, intricate

Museo de la Revolución

Museo de la Revolución

Cuba's former presidential palace, first occupied by the nation's third president, Mario Menocal in 1920, harbors an exhaustive history **museum** (Map p74, G2) whose exhibits tell a comprehensive, if unashamedly propagandist, story of Cuba's past, with a big focus on events post-1959.

The setting is more inspiring. The palace itself is an eclectic masterpiece with an interior furnished by the world-famous Tiffany's of New York. At the time of research, it was undergoing an interminable renovation with only the outdoor Pavillón Granma open. The alfresco area contains a replica of the yacht that carried Castro and 81 other revolutionaries from Mexico to Cuba in 1956 along with other vehicles associated with the revolution, including planes, rockets and a postal van used as a getaway vehicle during a 1957 attack.

wood- and ironwork, as well as an adjacent cafeteria and well-kept surrounding gardens. (teatromarti@patrimonio.ohc.cu)

Shopping

Memorias Librería   BOOKS

39 🏠 MAP P74, G3

A shop full of beautiful artifacts, the Memorias Librería was Havana's first genuine private antique bookstore, although it has since been joined by others. Delve into its gathered piles and you'll find wonderful rare collectibles, including old coins, postcards, posters, magazines and art deco signs from the 1930s. Priceless! (📞7-862-3153)

Plaza Carlos III   SHOPPING CENTER

40 🏠 MAP P74, B5

After Plaza América in Varadero, this is probably Cuba's flashiest shopping mall – and there's barely a tourist in sight. The place has taken a step up in recent years: formerly empty shelves are now at least half full of consumer goods. For something with a unique Cuban touch, pop into **Baracoa**, a chocolate shop.

Casa Guerlain   PERFUME

41 🏠 MAP P74, G2

Well, it's an interesting idea. This exclusive perfume parlor reopened on the same premises as the original 1917 shop and sells high-end perfume and cosmetics. But, really, who comes to Cuba to buy expensive scent?

Explore ◈
Vedado

Majestic, spread-out Vedado is Havana's once-notorious Mafia-run district. During Cuba's 50-year dalliance with the US, this was the city's commercial hub and in many ways it still is, although now the nightlife is less tawdry, the casinos have become discos and the hotels are as much historical relics as havens of luxury. Juxtaposed with modernist rascacielos (skyscrapers) is a leafy residential quarter.

The Short List

○ **Necrópolis Cristóbal Colón (p90)** *Walking among the dead in Latin America's finest cemetery.*

○ **Hotel Nacional (p92)** *Sipping Cuban cocktails at dusk on the terrace of Havana's emblematic hotel.*

○ **Plaza de la Revolución (p99)** *Soaking up the bombast in Cuba's hero-worshipping main square.*

○ **Fábrica de Arte Cubano (p106)** *Perusing art of the people, by the people, for the people in this veritable factory of creativity.*

○ **Jazz Club la Zorra y El Cuervo (p109)** *Exploring Havana's nighttime action in this legendary nightspot.*

Getting There & Around

🚌 Vedado is easily accessible from most other points in Havana, and numerous metro buses (with a 'P' prefix) converge on the neighborhood. The Habana Bus Tour T1 service stops at Plaza de la Revolución, Hotel Riviera and the Necrópolis Cristóbal Colón.

🚗 Taxis wait outside the main hotels, including the Hotel Nacional and Hotel Habana Libre.

Vedado Map on p96

Hotel Nacional (p92) JOEL VILLANUEVA/GETTY IMAGES ©

Top Experience 📷

Walk the Haunting Lanes of the Necrópolis Cristóbal Colón

Havana's gigantic cemetery is the finest in the Americas and rightly renowned for its striking religious iconography and elaborate marble statues. Far from being eerie, a walk within these 57 hallowed hectares can be an educational and emotional stroll through the annals of Cuban history. A detailed map is available at the entrance.

◉ MAP P96, C6

The Vital Statistics

Completed in 1871 using the designs of Spanish architect Calixto de Loira, the cemetery is one of the world's largest, harboring more than 450 mausoleums and 800,000 graves. Around 1.5 million living souls visit it annually, and around 50 people are buried here per day. Laid out in a perfect grid, the most important people are interred along the main avenues.

Puerta de la Paz

The main entrance, known as the Puerta de la Paz (Peace Gate), is framed by a splendid Byzantine-Romanesque triple arch that's topped by a statue of Our Lady of Mercy, carved by Cuban sculptor José Vilalta Saavedra in 1904.

Capilla Central

The neo-Romanesque Capilla Central (1886), in the exact center of the cemetery, is an unusual octagonal construction said to be modeled on Florence's Duomo. Rare is the day when you don't see at least one solemn funeral procession filing out of its hushed interior.

La Milagrosa

Northeast of the Capilla Central is the graveyard's most celebrated tomb, that of Señora Amelia Goyri, better known as La Milagrosa (the miraculous one), who died while giving birth in 1901. When the bodies were exhumed some years later, Amelia's body was uncorrupted, and the baby, who had been buried at its mother's feet, was allegedly found in her arms. As a result, La Milagrosa became the focus of a huge spiritual cult in Cuba, and thousands of people come here annually with gifts, in the hope of fulfilling dreams or solving problems. In keeping with tradition, pilgrims knock with the iron ring on the vault and walk away backwards when they leave.

★ **Top Tips**

o If you're short on time, stick to the main sights along Av Cristóbal Colón between the Puerta de la Paz and the Capilla Central.

o Detailed maps marked with all the important graves are available from the ticket office for a small fee.

o The cemetery is particularly beautiful and tranquil at sunset.

o Free guided tours leave regularly from the ticket office when there are enough people.

✕ **Take a Break**

There are a few basic cafes and eating joints outside the cemetery around the junction of Calle 23 and Calle 12.

A little further away, but worth the walk, is cool and trendy **Café Madrigal**.

Top Experience 📷

Sip a Mojito in the Hotel Nacional

Far more than just a hotel, the Nacional, built in 1930 as a copy of the Breakers Hotel in Palm Beach, Florida, is a national monument and one of Havana's architectural emblems. Even if you're not staying here, reserve time for a drink in the famous terrace bar overlooking the Malecón.

◉ MAP P96, G1

hotelnacionaldecuba.com

The Sergeants' Coup

The hotel's notoriety was cemented in October 1933 when, following a sergeants' coup by Fulgencio Batista that toppled the regime of Gerardo Machado, 300 aggrieved army officers took refuge in the building, hoping to curry favor with resident US ambassador Sumner Welles, who was staying there. Much to the officers' chagrin, Welles promptly left, allowing Batista's troops to open fire on the hotel, killing 14 officers and injuring seven. More were executed later, after they had surrendered.

The Havana Conference

In December 1946 the hotel gained infamy of a different kind when US mobsters Meyer Lansky and Lucky Luciano used it to host the largest ever get-together of the North American Mafia. The Cosa Nostra gathered here under the guise of a Frank Sinatra concert and convened a meeting that discussed Luciano's leadership, the growth of Mafia interests in Las Vegas and the potential of large-scale gambling in Cuba. In due course, Lansky went on to open up Havana's most luxurious casino in a refurbished wing of the hotel in 1955.

Facilities

The cherry on the cake of Cuban hotels and a flagship of the government-run Gran Caribe chain, the Hotel Nacional sports a hybrid of neoclassical, art deco and eclectic architectural styles. The richly tiled lobby is distinctly Moorish while the history-doused rooms are decorated with plaques advertising details of illustrious past occupants (Winston Churchill, Frank Sinatra and Errol Flynn among them). The towering Havana landmark also sports two swimming pools, a sweeping manicured lawn, a couple of lavish restaurants and its own top-class cabaret, the Parisién.

★ Top Tips

o Ask at reception about free hotel tours.

o Take a look at the 'Hall of Fame' in the ground-floor Bay View Bar.

o You haven't really been to Havana until you've sipped a mojito alfresco in the terrace bar overlooking the Straits of Florida.

o Look out for a small museum dedicated to the 1962 Cuban Missile Crisis set up in an old military battery in the hotel grounds.

✕ Take a Break

The hotel has numerous restaurants. The most economical is the 24-hour **Film Corner Cafetería** at basement level, which does great burgers (for Cuba) and milkshakes.

Walking Tour

Vedado by Night

Beneath the feted nightspots of Havana lies a parallel universe of less heavily promoted bars and venues, for which you may need a Spanish phrasebook, an 'in' with a Cuban amigo, or a mixture of luck and spontaneity to penetrate. Line your stomach, wise up on your cocktails and enjoy this nocturnal stroll (or – ahem – drunken stagger) around hidden Vedado.

Walk Facts

Start Coppelia

End Café Cantante Mi Habana

Length 4km; three to four hours

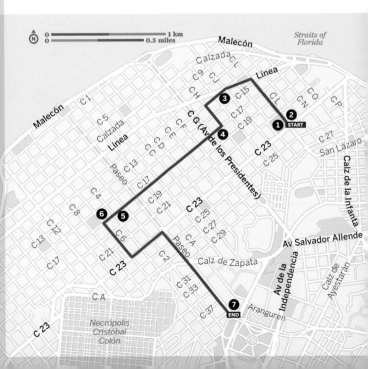

❶ Coppelia

Despite the ebb and flow of tourism in recent years, ice-cream parlor Coppelia, slap-bang in the middle of commercial Vedado, remains a quintessentially local stronghold. The intricacies of the queueing system can be confusing to unversed visitors, but with some Cuban pesos and a few words of Spanish you'll be warmly welcomed into the fold.

❷ Cine Yara

The Cine Yara is arguably Havana's finest movie house, host to many a Cuban date night, and a good place to get up to speed with the nation's dynamic film culture while fine-tuning your Spanish.

❸ Café Teatro Bertolt Brecht

Ask any young *habanero* where they go on Wednesday nights and they'll probably mention the 'Brecht' (📞7-832-9359), where long queues file patiently into an intimate theater to see genre-bending Cuban music collectives spin a couple of hours of melodic magic.

❹ El Hurón Azul

The home of the Union of Cuban Writers and Artists (Uneac), El Hurón Azul (uneac.org.cu) pulls in the local literati on Saturday nights for its long-standing *bolero* (ballad) shows. You can mingle freely with the pretentious and precocious in a grand Vedado mansion amid decorative architecture and rustling plants, with barely a tourist on the horizon.

❺ Café Madrigal

Vedado flirts with bohemia in this dimly lit gay-friendly bar (p91) that might have materialized from Paris' Latin Quarter in the days of James Joyce and Ernest Hemingway. Order a *tapita* (small tapa) and a cocktail, and retire to the atmospheric art nouveau terrace, where the buzz of nighttime conversation competes with the racket of vintage American cars rattling past below.

❻ Submarino Amarillo

No one knew much about Cuban *roqueros* (rock fans) until well into the 21st century. The groups that used to hang out clandestinely at the corner of Calles 23 and G have subsequently founded their own venue, Submarino Amarillo, a bar–live-music club with a bright-yellow interior that celebrates the Beatles but rocks to pretty much anything in 4/4 time.

❼ Café Cantante Mi Habana

Café Cantante Mi Habana (📞7-879-0710) is known as the best after-dark place to meet cool, fashion-conscious Cubans. This crowded but 'open' live-music and dancing venue inside the Teatro Nacional is known for its LGBTIQ+ parties.

N
0 _____ 500 m
0 _____ 0.25 miles

Straits of Florida

Malecón

Malecón

Calzada

Línea

Línea

Calzada

Río Almendares

Río Almendares

17
23
28
24
C 3
C 5
C 1
C 1
C 3
C 5
37
41
32
Paseo
20
C 2
36
34
C 4
C 6
44
C C
C B C 13
21
22
Centro Fidel Castro Ruz
2
C 11
C 15 C A
C 17
C 19
C 2
C 4
42
14
Paseo
C 21
33
C 6
C 8
C 10
4 Parque Lennon
Ruta Bikes
13
C 11
C 13
C 15
C 12
C 17 C 14
C 16 C 19 El Cimarrón
C 18
C 21
C 23
C 4
C 6
C 8
C 10
Calz de Zapata
43
Fábrica de Arte Cubano
15
C 20
C 22
C 23
C A
C 24
C 26
C 28
C 23

Necrópolis Cristóbal Colón

Calz de Zapata

San Antonio Chiquito

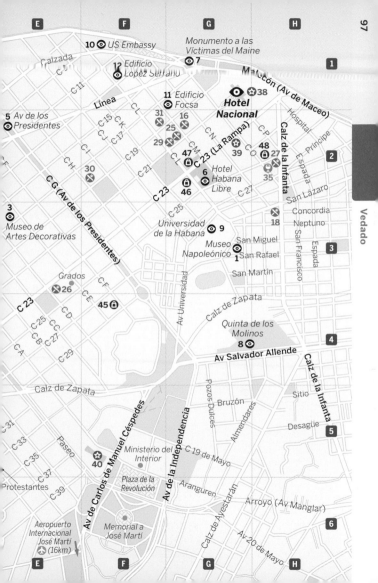

Vedado

E

F

G

H

Calzada

10 ⊙ US Embassy

Monumento a las
Víctimas del Maine

⊙ **7**

C 11

12 ⊙ Edificio
López Serrano

Malecón (Av de Maceo)

1

Línea

11 ⊙ Edificio
Focsa

⊙ ✸ **38**

5 Av de los
⊙ Presidentes

C 15 C K
C J C 17

31
⊗
25 ⊗
29 ⊗

16
⊗

C N

**Hotel
Nacional**

Hospital

Calz de la Infanta

E Príncipe

Espada

2

C I
C 19

C 21

C M

47 🔒
C L

C 23 (La Rampa)

⊙
39

48 ✸
⊙
27 🔒
⊗
35

San Lázaro

C-H

30
⊗

6 ⊙

Hotel
Habana
Libre

C 23
🔒
46

C 27

Espada
San Francisco

3
⊙

C 25

Museo de
Artes Decorativas

C G (Av de los Presidentes)

Universidad
de la Habana

⊙ **9**

Museo
Napoleónico
⊙
1

San Miguel

San Rafael

18
⊗

Concordia
Neptuno

3

San Martín

Grados

⊗**26**

C F

C E

Av Universidad

Calz de Zapata

C 23

C 25
C D
C B C 27
C A
C 29

45 🔒

Quinta de los
Molinos

8 ⊙

Av Salvador Allende

Calz de la Infanta

4

Calz de Zapata

Pozos Dulces

Bruzón

Almendares

Sitio

Desagüe

5

C 31

C 33

C 35

C 37

Paseo

Protestantes

C 39

✸
40

Av de Carlos de Manuel Céspedes

Ministerio del
Interior

Av de la Independencia

C 19 de Mayo

Aranguren

Calz de Ayestarán

Arroyo (Av Manglar)

6

Plaza de la
Revolución

Aeropuerto
Internacional
José Martí
✈ (16km)

Memorial a
José Martí

Av 20 de Mayo

E

F

G

H

Sights

Museo Napoleónico MUSEUM

1  MAP P96, G3

Without a doubt one of the best museums in Havana and thus in Cuba, this magnificently laid-out collection of 7000 objects associated with the life of Napoleon Bonaparte was amassed by Cuban sugar baron Julio Lobo and politician Orestes Ferrara.

Centro Fidel Castro Ruz CULTURAL CENTER

2 MAP P96, C3

Propagandist and proud of it, this superb museum and cultural center encased in a gorgeous eclectic mansion on Paseo Avenue offers an encyclopedic insight into the life and times of the man who ignited the Cuban Revolution. Objectivity isn't really the aim here. Instead, what you get is an uncritical homage to Fidel, beautifully laid out over two floors, a fecund garden and several affiliated buildings. (centrofidel.cu)

Museo de Artes Decorativas MUSEUM

3 MAP P96, E3

One of Havana's best museums dazzles like a European stately home. It's replete with all manner of architectural features, including rococo furniture, Chinese screens and an art deco bathroom. Equally interesting is the building itself, which is of French design and

Monumento a José Miguel Gómez

Plaza de la Revolución

Conceived by French urbanist Jean-Claude Forestier in the 1920s, the gigantic Plaza de la Revolución was part of Havana's 'new city,' which grew up between 1920 and 1959. Surrounded by gray, utilitarian buildings constructed in the late 1950s, the square today is the base of the Cuban government and a place where large-scale political rallies are held.

The ugly concrete block on the northern side of the plaza is the **Ministerio del Interior** (Map p96, F5), well known for its huge mural of Che Guevara with the words *Hasta la victoria siempre* (Always Toward Victory) emblazoned underneath.

Center stage in the plaza is the **Memorial a José Martí** (Map p96, F6), which at 138.5m was Havana's tallest structure until it was eclipsed by the K23 Tower in 2022.

was commissioned in 1924 by the wealthy Gómez family, who built the Manzana de Gómez shopping center in Centro Habana.

Parque Lennon   PARK

4 ◉ MAP P96, C4

If you prefer John Lennon to commie king Vladimir Lenin (both 20th-century personalities have a park named after them in Havana), decamp to this small square of green in Vedado, where a hyper-realistic statue of the former Beatle – unveiled by Fidel Castro on the 20th anniversary of Lennon's death – takes center stage.

Avenida de los Presidentes   MONUMENT

5 ◉ MAP P96, E2

Statues of illustrious Latin American leaders line the Parisian-style Calle G (officially known as Av de los Presidentes), including Salvador Allende (Chile), Benito Juárez (Mexico) and Simón Bolívar. At the top of the avenue is a huge marble **Monumento a José Miguel Gómez**, depicting Cuba's second president. At the other end, the monument to his predecessor – Cuba's first president, Tomás Estrada Palma (long considered a US puppet) – has been toppled, with just his shoes remaining on the original plinth.

Hotel Habana Libre   NOTABLE BUILDING

6 ◉ MAP P96, G2

This classic modernist hotel – the former Havana Hilton – was commandeered by Fidel Castro's revolutionaries in 1959 just nine months after it had opened, and promptly renamed the Habana Libre. During the first few months of the revolution, Castro ruled the country from a luxurious suite on the 24th floor. (melia.com/en/hotels/cuba/havana/tryp-habana-libre)

Monumento a las Víctimas del Maine   MONUMENT

7 ⊙ MAP P96, G1

West beyond the Hotel Nacional (p92) is a monument (1926) to the 266 American marines who were killed when the battleship USS *Maine* blew up mysteriously in Havana harbor in 1898. The American eagle that once sat on top was decapitated soon after the 1959 revolution. Despite rumors to this effect, its replacement in the form of a dove sculpted by Pablo Picasso never materialized.

Quinta de los Molinos   GARDENS

8 ⊙ MAP P96, G4

The former residence of Independence War general Máximo Gómez, this stately 'country house' sits in a lush, wooded park that has been managed as botanical gardens since 1839. The main house, called the Casa del Verano, opened as a museum in 2022 focusing mainly on Gómez' deeds in the Independence War of 1895–98.

Universidad de la Habana   UNIVERSITY

9 ⊙ MAP P96, G3

Founded by Dominican monks in 1728 and secularized in 1842, Havana's university began life in Habana Vieja before moving to its present site in 1902. The existing neoclassical complex dates from the second quarter of the 20th century, and today some 30,000 students take courses here in social sciences, humanities, natural sciences, mathematics and economics. (www.uh.cu/home)

US Embassy   LANDMARK

10 ⊙ MAP P96, F1

Arguably the world's most famous US embassy, this modernist seven-story building on the Malecón, with its high security fencing, first opened in 1953, but it closed abruptly in 1961 when the US and Cuba cut diplomatic relations. It reopened as the US Interests Section, set up by the Carter administration in 1977, and in July 2015 it was rebranded an embassy thanks to the political thaw instigated by the Obama administration. (cu.usembassy.gov)

Edificio Focsa   LANDMARK

11 ⊙ MAP P96, G1

Unmissable on the Havana skyline, the modernist Edificio Focsa was built between 1954 and 1956 in a record 28 months using pioneering computer technology. In 1999 it was listed as one of the seven modern engineering wonders of Cuba. With 39 floors housing 373 apartments, on its completion it was the second-largest concrete structure of its type in the world, built entirely without the use of cranes. (Focsa Bldg)

Understanding José Martí

'Two fatherlands have I, Cuba and the Night,' wrote poet, journalist, philosopher and all-round Renaissance man José Martí in 1882, perfectly summing up the dichotomies of late-19th-century Cuba, still as relevant today as they were 140 years ago.

Ironically, Martí – the brains behind Cuba's Second Independence War – remains the one figure who binds Cubans worldwide; a potent unifying force in a country fractiously divided by politics, economics and 145km of shark-infested ocean.

Born in Havana in 1853, Martí spent well over half his life outside the country he professed to love in sporadic exile, shunting between Spain, Guatemala, Venezuela and the US. But his absence hardly mattered. Martí's importance was in his words and ideas. An accomplished political commentator and a master of aphorisms, he was responsible in many ways for forming the modern Cuban identity and its dream of self-determination. It's difficult to meet a Cuban today who can't eloquently quote stanzas of his poetry. Similarly, there's barely a town or village across the country that doesn't have a statue or plaza named in his honor. The homage extends to the exile community in the US, where Cubans have named a radio station after him. Indeed, Martí is venerated across South and Central America, where he is often viewed as the ideological successor to Simón Bolívar.

A basic knowledge of Martí and his far-reaching influence is crucial to understanding contemporary Cuba. Havana, the city of his birth, is dotted with poignant monuments, but there are important sites elsewhere. The following are the bare essentials:

◦ **Memorial a José Martí** (p99) This giant tower (the second tallest in Havana) has a massive statue of El Maestro at its foot and a comprehensive museum inside.

◦ **Museo-Casa Natal de José Martí** (p49) Modest but lovingly curated birth house of Cuba's national hero.

Edificio López Serrano

LANDMARK

12 ◉ MAP P96, F1

Tucked away behind the US embassy is this art deco tower, which looks like the Empire State Building with the bottom 70 floors chopped off. One of Havana's first *rascacielos* (skyscrapers) when it was built in 1932, the López Serrano building now houses apartments.

Universidad de la Habana (p100)

Ruta Bikes · CYCLING

13 ⊙ MAP P96, B4

This was Havana's first decent bicycle-hire and -tour company when it started in 2013. Its cycling tours have proven to be consistently popular, particularly the three-hour classic city tour, which takes in the Bosque de la Habana, Plaza Vieja, Plaza de la Revolución and the Malecón. Book via phone or email at least a day ahead. Kids welcome. (rutabikes.com; 🚻)

Eating

Fangio Habana · INTERNATIONAL $$$

14 🍴 MAP P96, D4

This restaurant at Hotel Claxon, a private boutique accommodations in a handsome Vedado mansion on Paseo Avenue, focuses on an auto theme relating to erstwhile Argentinian racing driver Juan Fangio. The eating areas – garden, patio and rooftop terrace – are some of Havana's most romantic and the food is straight out of the top drawer of Cuban-international fusion. (claxonhotel.com)

El Cocinero · INTERNATIONAL $$$

15 🍴 MAP P96, A5

Located under the iconic smokestack of the Fábrica de Arte Cubano (p106), El Cocinero, not surprisingly, assembles some of Cuba's most creative dishes in either a gourmet restaurant or casual open terrace high above the rooftops of Vedado. The inventive around-the-world dishes (lamb curry, rabbit, duck confit) provide an attractive appetizer for Havana's best performance space next door. (elcocinerocuba.com/en)

Café Laurent INTERNATIONAL $$

16 MAP P96, G2

Occupying a 5th-floor suite of rooms with residential Vedado views, the unsigned Café Laurent is a sophisticated fine-dining restaurant encased, incongruously, in a glaringly ugly 1950s apartment block next to the Focsa building (p100). Starched white tablecloths, polished glasses and lacy drapes furnish the bright modernist interior, while seafood risotto and artistically presented pork sautéed with dry fruit and red wine headline the Cuban-Spanish menu. (7-832-6890)

Casa Mia Paladar CUBAN $$

17 MAP P96, C1

Rather than blinding you with fancy decor, clean-lined Casa Mia, abutting the Malecón, saves its surprises for the food; a simple menu that rests proudly on the classic foundations of Cuban cooking. The highlight in a medley of standouts is the cerdo cooked Pinar del Río style, which, as locals will tell you, is the melt-in-your-mouth pinnacle of Cuban pork. (❄)

El Biky CAFETERIA $

18 MAP P96, H3

Arriving like a breath of fresh air during the easing of economic restrictions in the early 2010s, Biky helped reinvent Havana's evolving brunch-lunch scene with its affordable quick-fire food, served in a modern cafe-restaurant hung with retro pre-revolution photos. It was so successful that it has since morphed into a 'gastronomic complex,' adding a cool bar and Havana's best bakery next door. (elbiky.com)

Ela y Paleta ICE CREAM $

19 MAP P96, D2

Mega popular ice-cream parlor with generous opening hours that is perennially packed with young Cubans filling up on equally generous scoops of ice cream. They'll even roll it for you Thai-style, although the crème de la crème is, arguably, the dulce-de-leche-flavored paletas (ice-cream popsicles). Look out for the bright pink building on an otherwise drab Vedado street.

Atelier CUBAN $$$

20 MAP P96, C2

The first thing that hits you at Atelier is the stupendous wall art: huge, thought-provoking, religious-tinged paintings. Equally arresting is the antique wooden ceiling that might have been ripped from a Mudejar church, plus the terra-cotta roof terrace and old-school elegance. Eventually you'll get around to the food: Cuban with a French influence and scribbled onto an ever-changing menu. (7-836-2025)

Decameron

INTERNATIONAL $$$

21 MAP P96, C3

Nondescript from the outside, but far prettier within – thanks largely to its famous collection of antique clocks (don't be late, now!) – the Decameron is a stalwart *paladar* (privately owned restaurant) that was always good, still is good and probably always will be good. The food is Cuban with international inflections. People rave about the savory tuna tart, risotto and swordfish. (🖊)

Café Eclectico

ITALIAN $$

22 MAP P96, C3

Affiliated to a chic boutique hotel on Paseo Avenue, Eclectico is part of a new Havana breed, reworking a three-story 1930s mansion into a place to be savored and enjoyed. The interior is bright, elegant and turquoise – lots of mirrors, glass and chandeliers – while the food is Italian with a few Cuban inflections. It's a dreamy spot for breakfast. (paseo206.com/restaurant)

La Chuchería

AMERICAN $

23 MAP P96, C2

Clinging to its perch close to the Malecón, this sleek sports bar looks as though it has floated across the straits from Florida like a returning exile. But what's run-of-the-mill in Miami is still vaguely exotic in Havana, as the tables of enthusiastic Cubans tucking into leafy salads, bumper sandwiches

El Cocinero (p102)

Farm-to-Table Restaurants

○ **El Cimarrón** (Map p96, C3,) Family-run farm-to-table restaurant and social project that hosts evening music and organizes cooking classes, El Cimarrón (the name means 'runaway enslaved person') wears many hats and succeeds on every level. There's a strong Afro-Cuban vibe in the art, bamboo furniture and percussive instruments, but the food's steadfastly *criolla,* with good vegetarian options.

○ **Grados** (Map p96, E3) A small but pioneering restaurant bivouacked in a family home in Vedado where the menu is never the same and enthusiastic chef-owner Raulito Bazuk conjures minor miracles out of whatever's available at any given time. Today, okra; tomorrow, creamed maize; the next day, who knows? There's a strong connection to local farms and Cuban ingredients.

and stupendous ice-cream milk-shakes attest.

Blue Moon   INTERNATIONAL $$

24 ⊗ MAP P96, D1

Formerly known as Opera but rebranded as Blue Moon (with the same owners) post-pandemic, this restaurant inhabits a colonnaded Vedado villa with head-turning art and operatic music. The food is equally dramatic and embraces the Italian 'Slow Food' philosophy, encompassing homemade gnocchi stuffed with yucca and rabbit cooked in Bucanero beer. ()

Cafetería Pilón   CAFE $

25 ⊗ MAP P96, G2

Havana was once something of a desert for desserts – bad news for travelers who can't live without a 4pm appointment with a slice of chocolate cake. But help has

arrived in the form of cafes such as Pilón, which are happy to fill those awkward dining gaps with brunches, all-day ice cream and the vitally important *merienda* (afternoon snack). (5-323-2552)

Topoly   IRANIAN $

26 ⊗ MAP P96, E3

Cuba finds solidarity with Iran in Havana's first and still *only* Iranian restaurant, corralled in a lovely colonnaded mansion on arterial Calle 23. Sit on the wraparound porch beneath iconic prints of Gandhi, José Martí and Che Guevara, and enjoy pureed eggplant, lamb *brochetas* (shish kebabs), fantastic coffee, and tea in ornate silver pots. (7-832-3224)

Toke Infanta y 25   BURGERS $

27 ⊗ MAP P96, H2

Buried amid the bruised edifices of Calzada de la Infanta on the

Fábrica de Arte Cubano

If only every city had a cultural venue as wide-ranging, inclusive and downright revolutionary as Havana's unique **art factory** (Map p96, A5; 📶). The 2014 brainchild of Cuban fusion musician X-Alfonso, this gallery–live-music venue–inspirational meeting place for anyone who can afford the modest entry fee is where electrifying 'happenings' take place in a cavernous, Bauhaus-like interior.

Repertoires are as flexible as they are creative. Expect everything from classical cellists to Cuban rappers to arty T-shirt designers selling their latest creations. It's more than exciting!

border of Vedado and Centro Habana, Toke is a simple cafe serving economical *hamburguesas* (hamburgers), strong coffee and chocolate brownies any time of the day or night. It's become known as a gay-friendly spot due to its location next to a couple of nightclubs.

Razones y Motivos   CUBAN $

28 ⊗ MAP P96, D1

This two-piece restaurant has an open terrace upstairs (Motivos) with a barbecue and a no-frills international menu, and an

air-conditioned space downstairs (Razones) plying slightly more upscale food, including steak. Neither is particularly fancy, and the reasonable prices attract a mainly Cuban clientele. The chefs do interesting things with lobster, flavoring it with pineapple sauce or coffee extract. (📞7-832-8732)

La Cocina de Esteban   INTERNATIONAL $$

29 ⊗ MAP P96, G2

A three-way explosion of Cuban, Italian and Spanish cuisine is guaranteed at this salubrious spot slap-bang in the middle of Vedado's hotel quarter. Bank on fine interpretations of risotto, pasta and grilled lobster. The venue is a regal mansion with inside and garden seating (and a fine rendition of Diego Velázquez' *Los borrachos* on the wall). (📞7-832-9649)

Restaurante Habana Blues   CUBAN $$

30 ⊗ MAP P96, F2

The dark, bluesy interior is backlit by a fabulous 3D mural of Havana's Morro castle (p61) and the waitstaff are all working actors from Cuban TV (check their caricature portraits in the entrance vestibule). First impressions set a high benchmark in this only-in-Havana restaurant that's popular with Cubans keen to enjoy economical plates of spicy prawns and caramelized ribs. (📞7-835-6545)

Ama
CAFE $

31  MAP P96, F2

Ama is a small, amicable catch-all cafe in Vedado near the Hotel Nacional that does its best to cater for vegetarians, vegans or anyone else with a distinctive food preference. The smoothies, salads, waffles and crepes all deserve an honorable mention. Seating is on an outside porch or indoors, where you'll also find a small shop displaying home-produced food items and small crafts. (📷)

Camino al Sol
VEGETARIAN $

32  MAP P96, B2

A decade ago Cuba and vegetarianism were about as compatible as Ronald Reagan and Leonid Brezhnev (ie not very), but tastes have developed and the times they are a changin'. The completely meat-free Camino al Sol, while still a rarity in Havana, makes imaginative quiches, soups, pies and house-made pasta, and displays them in a deli counter out front. (📷)

Drinking

Piano Bar Delirio Habanero
CLUB

This sometimes suave, sometimes frenetic lounge (see **40**  Map p96, F5), upstairs at Teatro Nacional de Cuba (p110), hosts everything from young rap artists to smooth, improvised jazz. The sharp red-accented bar and performance space abut a wall of glass overlooking Plaza de la Revolución – it's impressive at night with the

Fábrica de Arte Cubano

Memorial a José Martí (p99) and the handsome Che Guevara mural alluringly backlit. (📞7-878-4275)

Bar-Restaurante 1830 CLUB

33 MAP P96, A4

If you want to salsa dance, this is *the* place to go: after the Sunday-night show, literally everyone takes to the floor. It's at the far-western end of the Malecón with a water-facing terrace. Skip the food.

Pazillo Bar BAR

34 MAP P96, B3

The name Pazillo (a pun on the word passageway/corridor) doesn't really do justice to this funky haunt that has provided a second coming for a handsome Vedado villa. A chic little passageway is augmented by a cool bar, neon-fringed lounge and communal outdoor seating area. Live jazz is a regular feature and the super-sized 'snacks' help soak up the copious cocktails.

Cabaret Las Vegas CLUB

35 MAP P96, H2

The Vegas was once a rough and slightly seedy local music dive, but these days it's better known for its late-night drag shows and is one of Havana's most reliable gay clubs.

Cabaret Parisién

Juguera de 6
JUICE BAR

36 MAP P96, B2

Tucked behind a residential building in sight of the Hotel Meliá Cohiba , this small walk-up bar offers an astounding 97 fresh juice combinations using the best tropical-fruit flavors (including papaya, mango and pineapple) and sometimes vegetables, too. You can stand around with the locals and detox from last night's deep-fried pork for a few dollars a glass.

Bar-Club Imágenes
BAR

37 MAP P96, C2

This small, darkly lit piano bar attracts something of an older Cuban crowd with its regular diet of *boleros* and *trova* (traditional music), though there are also comedy shows; check the schedule posted outside.

Entertainment

Cabaret Parisién
CABARET

38 MAP P96, H1

One rung down from Marianao's world-famous Tropicana (p125), but way cheaper and closer to the city center, the nightly Cabaret Parisién in the Hotel Nacional (p92) is well worth a look, especially if you're staying in or around Vedado. It's the usual mix of frills, feathers and scantily clad dancers, but the choreography is first-class and the costumes wonderfully flamboyant. (hotelnacionaldecuba.com)

Favorite Places to Eat

Cradoc Comfort food in a place that's chic but also a bit like your mother's house. There's usually a tasting menu with interesting ingredients like *crema de maíz* (creamed corn) and okra. (p105)

Antojos I would recommend the croquettes, the *tostones con lechón* (fried plantain with suckling pig) and the fish cooked on the BBQ. (p51)

Chachacha Very Cuban ambience, and food, live music and great art on the walls.

El Café A place where you can create your own brunch. It's also a good spot for vegetarians and vegans. (p56)

El Antonia Good live music in the evenings. (p54)

Recommended by Celine Terry, owner of Residencia Albero Dulce (alberodulce. com), a boutique hotel and yoga center near Plaza de la Revolución

Jazz Club la Zorra y El Cuervo
LIVE MUSIC

39 MAP P96, G2

One of several long-standing and highly lauded jazz clubs, the Vixen and the Crow opens its doors nightly at 10pm to long lines of committed music fiends. Enter through a red British phone box and descend into a diminutive and dark basement. The scene is invariably hot and clamorous and leans toward freestyle jazz. (☎7-833-2402)

Teatro Nacional de Cuba
THEATER

40 ⭐ MAP P96, F5

One of the twin pillars of Havana's cultural life, the Teatro Nacional de Cuba on Plaza de la Revolución is the modern rival to the Gran Teatro (p76) in Centro Habana. Built in the 1950s as part of Jean-Claude Forestier's grand city expansion, the complex hosts landmark concerts, foreign theater troupes and La Colmenita children's company. (☎7-879-6011)

Habana Café
CABARET

41 ⭐ MAP P96, B2

A hip and trendy nightclub-cabaret show at the **Hotel Meliá Cohiba** (meliacuba.com), laid out in 1950s American style but with live salsa music. After 1am the tables are cleared and the place rocks to 'international music' until the cock crows. Excellent value.

Casa de la Amistad
LIVE PERFORMANCE

42 ⭐ MAP P96, D4

This elegant pink mansion built in 1926 by Juan Pedro Baró, a rich landowner involved in a scandalous marriage with high-society belle Catalina Lasa, is the unlikely nexus of Havana's blossoming rock-and-roll scene. House bands play here on Sunday night at 6:30pm to a usually adoring audience of multigenerational *roqueros*. (☎7-830-3114)

El Turquino
LIVE MUSIC

On the 25th floor of the Hotel Habana Libre (p99), this well-known club (see 6 ◉ Map p96, G2) puts on mediocre cabaret shows followed by much better live bands and dancing. The pièce de résistance is the retractable roof, which slides back when everyone hits the dance floor around midnight.

Cine Charles Chaplin
CINEMA

43 ⭐ MAP P96, C5

One of Cuba's largest and best-equipped cinemas, the Chaplin shows nightly films of all types and sometimes runs a special season on one director. The lobby is a veritable museum of Cuban film posters and is worth a look at any time of day. (☎7-831-1101)

Teatro Mella
THEATER

44 ⭐ MAP P96, D3

Occupying the site of the old Rodi Cinema on Línea, Teatro Mella offers one of Havana's most comprehensive programs, including an international ballet festival, comedy shows, theater, dance and intermittent performances from the famous Conjunto Folklórico Nacional. American rock band Blondie played here in 2019. (☎7-833-8696)

Teatro Mella

Shopping

Bazar Estaciones
GIFTS & SOUVENIRS

45  MAP P96, F4

This lovingly curated private shop sells some interesting and unique souvenirs (not the standard government-branded stuff). Think creative lamps, framed photos, cute cards and old vinyl made into clocks. It's just off Av de los Presidentes opposite the grand José Miguel Gómez monument. (☏7-832-9965)

La Habana Sí
GIFTS & SOUVENIRS

46 MAP P96, G2

This government-run ARTex shop opposite the Hotel Habana Libre

(p99) has a good selection of books, crafts, cards and other only-in-Cuba souvenirs.

Andare – Bazar de Arte
GIFTS & SOUVENIRS

47 MAP P96, G2

A selection of old movie posters, antique postcards, T-shirts and, of course, all the greatest Cuban films on videotape are sold at this state-run shop next to the Cine Yara (p95).

Librería Centenario del Apóstol
BOOKS

48 MAP P96, H2

Great assortment of used books with a José Martí bias in downtown Vedado.

Explore
Playa & Marianao

Playa, west of Vedado across the Río Almendares, is a large, complex municipality. For the sake of clarity, it can be split into several contrasting subneighborhoods. Most of the sights are centered in Miramar, a leafy diplomatic quarter of broad avenues, geriatric banyan trees and fine private restaurants. Further west lies Marina Hemingway, Havana's premier, if slightly decrepit, boat marina.

The Short List

○ **Otramanera (p115)** *Trying out new flavors at one of Havana's leading private restaurants, housed in a cool garden residence in Miramar.*

○ **Marina Hemingway (p118)** *Following the Hemingway legend at the marina named after him with boating and fishing trips.*

○ **El Bosque de la Habana (p119)** *Walking or cycling through the wooded trails that track the Río Almendares.*

○ **Tropicana Nightclub (p125)** *Catching a show at the ultimate Cuban cabaret, which has been demonstrating its feathers, exotic headwear and athletic dancing panache since 1939.*

Getting There & Around

🚌 The best way to get to Playa from Centro Habana and Vedado is on Habana Bus Tour T1 service, which plies most of the neighborhood's highlights all the way to La Cecilia on Av 5 in Cubanacán. From here the less reliable T2 bus connects to Marina Hemingway four times a day. Check ahead.

Playa & Marianao Map on p116

Rio Jaimanitas from Santy Pescador (p122) HEMIS/ALAMY STOCK PHOTO ©

Walking Tour 🥾

Unsignposted Playa

Playa doesn't always advertise its best bits. Call it confidence, arrogance, negligence or whatever, but the neighborhood guards a rich raft of secrets that are worth seeking out.

Walk Facts

Start El Bosque de la Habana

End Iglesia Jesús de Miramar

Length 7km; three hours

❶ El Bosque de la Habana

First things first: this is no mani-cured European park with gravel walkways and shapely shrubs, and you won't find many tourists here. However, as an ecological revitalization project El Bosque de la Habana is important. It's also a sacred Santería site, where ad-herents often leave ritual offerings beneath the trees.

❷ Otramanera

Secluded behind a high fence from the jovial street life of Miramar, Otramanera ('another way') is a legitimate contender for Havana's best restaurant. With its minimalist ranch-house setting and romanti-cally lit garden bar, it might have materialized from LA, while the Cuban-Spanish food – truffled quail eggs, rabbit stew – is New York standard and all the more re-markable considering the difficulty in securing ingredients.

❸ Espacios

When the *au courant* tapas bar–chill-out lounge of Espacios (☏7-202-2921) opened in the early 2010s, it built up its reputation by word of mouth. There's no sign outside the large detached house it inhabits in Miramar. Instead, you have to know someone hip enough to have been there to find out the address.

❹ Quinta Avenida

Before the revolution, Miramar was a posh residential quarter where Cuba's richest people lived in huge, ostentatious mansions. Today, the dizzying cavalcade of fine eclectic architecture along arterial Quinta Avenida (Av 5) is home to embassies and state-run businesses.

❺ Café Fortuna Joe

There are two Café Fortunas in Miramar, both pretty outlandish, but only this **Fortuna** (☏5-413-3706) has the suffix 'Joe.' That Fortuna inhabits a two-story beach house on Av 1, and inside you can enjoy some of Havana's best cof-fee in some of its weirdest seating, including a horse carriage, a boat and a decommissioned toilet!

❻ Paseo Maritimo 1ra y 70

This slightly ramshackle water-side park sits in front of the large, ultra-modern Gran Muthu Hotel at the western end of Miramar's diplo district. It consists of a cluster of privately run beach-shack-style restaurants that serve a variable inventory of seafood with sides of live music that can go on well into the *madrugada* (small hours).

❼ Iglesia Jesús de Miramar

Miramar's church doesn't ap-pear much in Havana's potted sights. People who've never been here consider it too modern, too peripheral and too ordinary. But the church's true glory is within: 14 giant Stations of the Cross painted in resplendent detail across the walls.

Playa & Marianao

Straits of Florida

A · **B** · **C** · **D** · **E** · **F**

0 — 1 km
0 — 0.5 miles

PLAYA

MIRAMAR

Av 5
Av 3
Av 1
Av 5

La Maqueta de la Capital

Parque Miramar

Memorial de la Denuncia

Casa de las Tejas Verdes

VEDADO

C 23

KOHLY

NUEVO VEDADO

Parque Almendares

El Bosque de la Habana

Río Almendares

Acuario Nacional

Russian Embassy

Fundación Naturaleza y El Hombre

Parque Monte Barreto

BUENA VISTA

Universidad de las Artes

CUBANACÁN

Ciudad Libertad Airport

Ciudad Libertad

Museo de la Alfabetización

Av 41

For reviews see	
◎ Sights	p117
✪ Eating	p120
✪ Entertainment	p125
🛍 Shopping	p126

Sights

Memorial de la Denuncia
MUSEUM

1 ◉ MAP P116, F1

The former Museum of the Ministry of the Interior was remodeled in 2017 to form this far more interesting (if propaganda-ridden) look at US actions against Cuba in the last 60+ years. The entrance stairway is covered with more than 3000 crosses, denoting people killed in skirmishes involving the US or other foreign powers since 1959, from the Bay of Pigs to the 1976 bomb aboard Cubana flight 455. (☎7-203-0120)

Acuario Nacional
AQUARIUM

2 ◉ MAP P116, D1

Founded in 1960, the national aquarium is a Havana institution designed primarily for Cuban visitors, who arrive by the legion. Overseas visitors, be warned: the rather dilapidated facilities and limited selection of things to see are not on par with aquariums elsewhere. Sea turtles are the specialty, but there are also sea lions, crocs and dolphins, including hourly dolphin shows. Note that dolphin performances are widely criticized by animal-welfare groups, who say that captivity for such complex marine mammals is debilitating and stressful. (acuarionacional.cu/wifi; 🚹)

Russian Embassy
LANDMARK

3 ◉ MAP P116, C1

In case you were wondering, that huge Stalinist obelisk that dominates the skyline halfway down Av Quinta is the Russian (formerly Soviet) embassy, testament to the days when Fidel Castro liked to hobnob with Brezhnev et al.

Club Habana
HISTORIC BUILDING

4 ◉ MAP P116, A1

This fabulously eclectic 1928 mansion in Flores once housed the Havana Biltmore Yacht & Country Club. These days the establishment has swung full circle and it is again a popular hangout for diplomats and affluent visitors. The club has its own well-raked beach (technically the closest to central Havana), swimming pools (note plural), bar and restaurant, all open to non-members for a fee. (☎7-204-5700)

Universidad de las Artes
NOTABLE BUILDING

5 ◉ MAP P116, A2

The leading art academy in Cuba was established in the former Havana Country Club in 1961 and elevated to the status of institute in 1976. The cluster of buildings – some unfinished, some half-restored, but all gloriously graceful with unusual arches, domes and red brick – was the brainchild of Che Guevara and a team of architects. (isa.cult.cu)

La Maqueta de la Capital

MUSEUM

6 ⦿ MAP P116, E1

Havana itself is somewhat dilapidated in parts and so, ironically, is this huge 1:1000 scale model of the city, which looks as though it could do with a good dusting. The model was created for urban-planning purposes but is now a tourist attraction. It's going through a protracted (interminable) renovation but can usually still be viewed.

Marina Hemingway

MARINA

7 ⦿ MAP P116, A1

Havana's premier marina was constructed in 1953 in the small coastal community of Santa Fé. After the revolution it was nationalized and named after Fidel Castro's favorite *Yanqui*. The marina has four 800m-long channels, a dive center, a motley collection of shops and restaurants, and two hotels, and is only worth visiting if you're docking your boat or organizing water-sports activities. (cubanautica.travel/en/destinos /la-habana)

Fundación Naturaleza y El Hombre

MUSEUM

8 ⦿ MAP P116, C2

This tiny museum seems to confirm the adage 'small is beautiful.' It displays artifacts from a 17,422km canoe trip from the Amazon source to the sea that was led by Cuban intellectual and anthropologist António Núñez Jiménez in 1987. Exhibits among the

Russian Embassy (p117)

El Bosque de la Habana

Running along the banks of the Río Almendares, below the bridge on Calle 23, is this welcome oasis of greenery and fresh air in the heart of the chaotic city (Map p116, E4). The 'Bosque' might not be the Bois de Boulogne (witness the stray dogs and unsightly litter), but it is a work in progress and far healthier than it was in the 1990s.

The lower park (closer to the bridge) is usually called **Parque Almendares** and is more developed, with a stash of so-so facilities, including an antiquated miniature golf course, the Anfiteatro Parque Almendares (a small outdoor performance space) and a kids' playground. South of the bridge, the so-called **Parque Metropolitano** is wilder and more bewitching, with giant trees shrouded by hanging curtains of vines. Several paths wind their way through the greenery between the road and the river, and Santería ceremonies are sometimes performed here. It's a beguiling spot, and potentially even more so if the city can sort out the litter problem.

astounding array of items include one of Cuba's largest photography collections, books written by the prolific Núñez Jiménez, his beloved canoe and a famous portrait of Fidel Castro by Ecuadorian painter Oswaldo Guayasamín. (fanj.cult.cu)

Museo de la Alfabetización   MUSEUM

9 ◉ MAP P116, B4

The former Cuartel Colombia military airfield at Marianao is now a school complex called **Ciudad Libertad**. Pass through the gate to visit this inspiring museum, which describes the 1961 literacy campaign during which 100,000 youths aged 12 to 18 spread out across Cuba to teach reading and writing to farmers, workers and seniors.

Marlin Náutica   WATER SPORTS

10 ◉ MAP P116, A1

Marlin Náutica at Marina Hemingway runs four-hour deep-sea-fishing trips for four anglers for around US$330, including tackle and an open bar; marlin season is June to October. Catamaran tours of Havana's littoral are also available (four-person minimum). (marinasmarlin.com/home)

La Aguja Marlin Diving Center   DIVING

11 ◉ MAP P116, A1

Between Marlin Náutica and the shopping center at Marina Hemingway, this center offers scuba diving, resort dive courses and full-blown qualifications. Departures are at 9am and head out to water around Havana. A diving excursion

A Classic Miramar House

Emerging from the tunnel under the Río Almendares, your first glimpse of Miramar is the so-called **Casa de las Tejas Verdes** (Map p116, F2; tejasverdes@patrimonio.ohc.cu). A subtle hint of the eclecticism to come: the House of the Green Tiles is the only example of Queen Anne architecture in Cuba. The house was built in 1926, and for most of its existence was the home of a semi-famous Havana socialite, Luisa Rodríguez Faxas, who lived here from 1943 to 1999.

After Faxas' death the house was passed to the Cuban government, which restored it and opened the building as an architectural study center in 2010. It's not strictly a museum, but management runs free tours on Wednesdays at 10am or by appointment at other times; phone ahead on 7-212-5282.

to Playa Girón, where the diving's much better, can also be arranged. (marinasmarlin.com/home)

Eating

Sensaciones   INTERNATIONAL $$$

12 🌍 MAP P116, C2

One of a new breed of Miramar *paladares* (private restaurants), Sensaciones inhabits a subtly elegant building with indoor and balcony seating, a charcoal grill, a small, streamlined bar and tasteful minimalist decor. The food's equally thoughtful: a mix of lighter bites (empanadas, croquettes, ceviche), expertly grilled steak and fish, and super-smooth piña coladas. Sensations? You'll have a few.

Nero di Seppia   ITALIAN $$$

13 🌍 MAP P116, F1

In the bun-fight for the best Italian restaurant in Havana, Nero di Seppia is a front-runner courtesy of its Naples-quality pizza crust, daily homemade pasta and Turin-worthy cappuccinos. High standards have been maintained despite Cuba's current economic woes and you can still bank on eggplant, a variety of cheeses, cured ham and medium-rare steak. No surprise, the owner's Italian.

La Esperanza   INTERNATIONAL $$$

14 🌍 MAP P116, F1

La Esperanza recalls those old-school *paladar* days when you felt you were dining in someone's home (you kinda are!). The interior of this vine-covered house is a riot of quirky antiques, old portraits and refined 1940s furnishings, while the food includes such exquisite dishes as *pollo luna de miel* (chicken flambéed in rum) and lamb brochettes. (📞7-202-4361)

La Casa del Gelato

ICE CREAM $

15 MAP P116, D1

One of a growing number of privately run ice-cream makers in Havana, this was one of the first in on the act and it's still one of the best. Unlike those closer to the city center, it has plenty of seating inside and out and, in addition to a rich array of flavors, it sells cakes, sandwiches and strong coffee. (❄)

Paladar Vista Mar

SEAFOOD $$$

16 MAP P116, E1

The Vista Mar is one of half a dozen or so Havana *paladares* that have been around since the 1990s, and it continues to excel despite newer competition. It inhabits a 1950s-era family home, facing the ocean and embellished by a beautiful infinity pool. The food is upmarket but classic, featuring ceviche, octopus and pork loin. (7-203-8328)

Toros y Tapas

SPANISH $$$

17 MAP P116, F1

Memories of the old country will come flooding back in this unashamedly Spanish restaurant with *garbanzos fritos* (fried chickpeas), whole grilled fish, paella, *tortilla* (omelet) and *mucho más*. The decor is similarly evocative: matador's capes, bullfighting posters and even some bullish taxidermy. Vegetarians need not apply.

Santy Pescador (p122)

Santy Pescador

SEAFOOD $$

18 MAP P116, A2

It's all about fish at the 'The Holy Fisherman,' a waterside joint wedged between Marina Hemingway and Fusterlandia that's one of the few decent options in this neck of the woods. You can sit on a covered deck overlooking the modest fishing fleet and sample unusual-for-Cuba dishes like ceviche and sushi, or old stalwarts such as prawns and lobster.

La Catrina

MEXICAN $$

19 MAP P116, B1

Specialized Mexican restaurants are still a surprising rarity in Cuba despite many local places absorbing tacos onto their menus. So, all hail to Catrina for sticking its head above the parapet and introducing *habaneros* to the real deal – tacos on a slate, fajitas, quesadillas, burritos and more. The decor includes bright color accents, the odd skull, and a choice of indoor and outdoor seating.

La Corte del Príncipe

ITALIAN $$$

20 MAP P116, C2

An out-of-the-way location has never seemed to hinder La Corte, which has developed a loyal following over the years – Mick Jagger and the Pope among them. The reason? It's one of the most authentic Italian joints in town, serving homemade pasta, eggplant parmigiana, epic prawns and focaccia (but not pizza). It even keeps

El Bosque de la Habana

Italian hours, closing briefly for an afternoon siesta. (📞5-255-9091)

El Aljibe
CARIBBEAN $$

21 ✖ MAP P116, E2

Aljibe is a legend in Havana: a restaurant whose original incarnation predated the revolution and whose second coming in the 1990s revived its most renowned dish, the obligatory *pollo 'El Aljibe'* (roast chicken in a bitter-orange sauce), served with as-much-as-you-can-eat helpings of white rice, black beans, fried plantain, French fries and salad. (📞7-204-1583/4)

28th & Mar
DINER $

22 ✖ MAP P116, E1

Diner-style dishes whisked swiftly to your table in an old one-story beach house on Av 1 with the ocean crashing mere meters from the door. Scour the menu for decadent vanilla milkshakes and bread rolls so crispy you'll need a broom to sweep the floor afterwards.

El Tocororo
CARIBBEAN $$$

23 ✖ MAP P116, E1

Once considered one of Havana's finest government-run restaurants, along with El Aljibe, El Tocororo has lost ground to new private competition in recent years and is often criticized as overpriced. Nonetheless, the candlelit tables and grandiose interior make a visit worthwhile, while the menu, with such luxuries as lobster tail and

Top Spots for Artsy Photos

The streets of Havana, especially Calle San Lázaro and Calle Cárdenas for their textures and diverse architecture where you can find expressive faces for portraits.

El Bosque de la Habana for its enigmatic vegetation.

The old bars from the 1950s that you find in Calle Neptuno in Centro Habana for their throwback charm.

The central train station of Havana for its monochromatic diversity.

Recommended by **Joanne Marina Soto Fernandez,** *a photographer based in Playa, Havana.* @titinastyle

pepper steak, still has the ability to surprise. (📞7-202-4530)

Siete Días
INTERNATIONAL $$

24 ✖ MAP P116, F1

This seaside spot has a very decent menu, but it's really the ambience, location and view that make it so memorable. Housed in a beautiful mansion, the outdoor dining room-bar sits on Playa de 16, a lovely city beach known to anyone who grew up in Havana. It's a perfect place to watch

Playa's Subneighborhoods ⇥

The municipality of Playa encompasses half a dozen smaller districts. To fully appreciate it you'll need to cover a lot of ground either on foot, or in short hops by bus or taxi.

The obvious starting point is **Miramar**, the tree-lined diplomatic quarter that begins just across the Río Almendares from Vedado. Quinta Avenida (Av 5) is Miramar's main drag. Rather like Paseo de Martí (Prado) in Centro Habana, it has a broad central walkway. Eating and drinking places and many of the main sights lie either on Av 5 or a few blocks to the north and south. Some of the best restaurants are hidden away in quiet side streets but are worth seeking out.

Most of Playa's large hotels are located in a rectangular block shoehorned between Calles 60 and 84. Beyond them Miramar fades into **Cubanacán**, Havana's one-time Beverly Hills, now known for its convention centers and yacht club.

Things get posher still in the subneighborhood of **Flores**, home of the opulent Club Habana (p117) and – ironically – Playa's only real beach. Just west of Flores is **Jaimanitas**, more working class and a one-time fishing village that, since the 1990s, has gradually transformed itself into Havana's finest street-art project, Fusterlandia. Western Playa ends in **Santa Fé**, which hosts Havana's largest marina (p118), named after Ernest Hemingway.

Marianao is usually only visited for its world-famous Tropicana Nightclub. Less heralded is the **Ciudad Libertad**, a former military barracks that Fidel Castro made into a massive school campus. It's now the home of the Museo de la Alfabetización (p119).

the sunset with a drink in hand. (☏7-209-6889)

under the breezy front canopy. (☏7-204-4232)

Pan.com   FAST FOOD $

25 🍴 MAP P116, E2

In McDonald's-free Havana, Pan.com is about as fast as food gets. This small, state-run Cuban chain does hearty sandwiches (on proper Cuban bread!), cheap burgers and ice-cream milkshakes to die for. Join the diplomats

Casa Española   SPANISH $$

26 🍴 MAP P116, E2

A medieval parody built in the Batista era by the silly-rich Gustavo Gutiérrez y Sánchez, this crenellated castle in Miramar has found new life as a Spanish-themed food complex cashing in on the Don Quixote legend. There are three options here: a restaurant, a cafe and a barbecue. The former is the most consciously Spanish, serving paella straight from the pan. (📞 7-206-9644)

Papa's Complejo Turístico

CARIBBEAN $$

27 ❌ MAP P116, A2

There's all sorts of stuff going on at this joint at Marina Hemingway, from beer-swilling boatmen to *American Idol* wannabes hogging the karaoke machine. The eating options are equally varied, with a posh Chinese place (with dress code) and an outdoor *ranchón* (rustic, open-sided restaurant).

Entertainment

Tropicana Nightclub

CABARET

28 ⭐ MAP P116, C4

An institution since its 1939 opening, the world-famous Tropicana was one of the few bastions of Havana's Las Vegas–style nightlife to survive the revolution. Immortalized in Graham Greene's 1958 *Our Man in Havana,* the open-air cabaret show here has changed little since its 1950s heyday, with flamboyantly clad dancers running through a potted history of Cuban music on a multilevel stage. (cabaret-tropicana.com/en)

Casa de la Música

LIVE MUSIC

29 ⭐ MAP P116, E2

Launched with a concert by renowned jazz pianist Chucho

Valdés in 1994, this Miramar favorite is run by national Cuban recording company EGREM, and the programs are generally a lot more authentic than the cabaret entertainment you'll see at the hotels. It's a little more suave than its Centro Habana namesake. (📞 7-202-6147)

Café Miramar

LIVE MUSIC

30 ⭐ MAP P116, B1

A suitably refined little club for a suitably refined part of Playa, this venue encased in the Cine Teatro Miramar and affiliated with government agency ARTex is dedicated mainly to live jazz, although other elements (such as funk) are sometimes thrown into the mix. Things usually get jamming at 9pm-ish and there's cheap food.

Teatro Karl Marx

LIVE MUSIC

31 ⭐ MAP P116, F1

Size-wise the Karl Marx puts other Havana theaters in the shade, with a seating capacity of 5500 in a single auditorium. The very biggest events happen here, such as the closing galas for the jazz and film festivals, and rare concerts by *trovadores* such as Silvio Rodríguez. (📞 7-209-1991)

Don Cangrejo

LIVE MUSIC

32 ⭐ MAP P116, F1

The daytime restaurant of the Cuban fisheries becomes party central, particularly on Friday night, with alfresco live music (often by big-name acts) and an atmosphere akin to that of an undergraduate freshers' ball. It's crowded and there are queues.

La Cecilia   LIVE MUSIC

33 ⭐ MAP P116, A1

This walled outdoor garden complex serves traditional Cuban food and keeps tour groups hydrated with mojitos, but it's best known for its big-band salsa music, which blasts out on weekend nights beneath the ferns and canopies. (📞7-204-1562)

Club Almendares   DANCE

34 ⭐ MAP P116, F3

Go into the woods in El Bosque de la Habana for the weekly **Fiesta del Casino** (p119), a popular open-air disco where a mix of Cubans and non-Cubans come to dance salsa. The event starts with a communal salsa lesson from **Club Salseando Chévere** (salseandochevere.com). (📞7-204 4990)

Circo Trompoloco   CIRCUS

35 ⭐ MAP P116, A1

Havana's permanent 'Big Top,' with a weekend matinee featuring strongmen, contortionists and acrobats. (circonacionaldecuba.cu; 👥)

Salón Rosado
Benny Moré   LIVE MUSIC

36 ⭐ MAP P116, E3

If you're looking for something inherently Cuban, tag along with the local *habaneros* for some very *caliente* action at this outdoor venue known colloquially as La Tropical. The long-standing club hosts live music and has changed its spots over the years – these days it's less Benny Moré and more jazz, with occasional reggaeton thrown in. (📞7-206-1281)

Shopping

La Casa del
Habano Quinta   CIGARS

37 🔒 MAP P116, F2

Arguably Havana's top cigar store – and there are many contenders. The primary reasons: it's well-stocked, with well-informed staff, a comfy smoking lounge and a decent on-site restaurant. It also enjoys the on-off presence of many of Cuba's top cigar aficionados. (habanos.com)

Salomé Casa
de Modas   CLOTHING

38 🔒 MAP P116, E1

Every single piece at this private boutique reflects authentic Cuban style. It specializes in all things linen – dresses, blouses, trousers and *guayaberas* (men's shirts). Salomé's pieces are elegant but unpretentious, featuring pastel colors, pleats and embroidery. (salomemodas@hotmail.com)

Tropicana Nightclub (p125)

La Maison
CLOTHING

39 🔒 MAP P116, F2

The Cuban fashion fascination is in high gear at this small boutique complex hidden in a Miramar villa. It has a limited selection of designer clothing, shoes, handbags, jewelry and cosmetics but is best known for its fashion shows (Thursday to Sunday) that take place on a leafy back patio.

Miramar Trade Center
SHOPPING CENTER

40 🔒 MAP P116, C1

Cuba's largest and most modern shopping and business center houses myriad stores, airline offices and embassies. Look out for the offbeat art installations, including a herd of elephants prancing through.

Egrem Tienda de Música
MUSIC

41 🔒 MAP P116, F1

There's a small CD outlet hidden here in a quiet Miramar avenue, at the site of Havana's most celebrated recording studios.

Worth a Trip 🔭
Embrace the Avant-Garde at Fusterlandia

Where does art go after Antoni Gaudí? For a hint, head west from central Havana to the seemingly low-key district of Jaimanitas, where artist José Fuster has turned his home neighborhood into a masterpiece of intricate tile work and kaleidoscopic colors that makes Barcelona's Park Güell look positively sedate. Imagine Gaudí with a Cuban accent relocated to a tropical setting.

Neighborhood Sign

Welcoming you to the Fusterlandia 'show' is the Jaimanitas neighborhood sign, with the words 'Homenaje a Gaudí' (Homage to Gaudí) arranged in a vivid mosaic. From here, Fuster's surrealistic ceramics cover several city blocks, encompassing park benches, public spaces and more than 120 local houses. Bus stops, street signs and even a doctor's surgery have all been given an artistic makeover.

Taller-Estudio José Fuster

The centerpiece of the project is Fuster's own house. Multilevel Taller-Estudio José Fuster (☎ 5-281-5421) is decorated from roof to foundations with art, sculpture and – above all – mosaic tiles of every color and description. The overall impression defies written expression (just GO!): the place is a fantastical mishmash of spiraling walkways, giant hands, cowboys with cartoonish faces, and sunburst motifs arranged around a small pool. The work mixes elements of Pablo Picasso and Gaudí with stylized snippets of Paul Gauguin, Wifredo Lam, magic realism, maritime influences and aspects of the Santería religion.

The Bus Stops

There's no mistaking Fusterlandia's disembarkation point for visitors arriving by bus. Two local stops on either side of Quinta Avenida (Av 5) have been given the full Fuster treatment, with curvaceous profiles, toadstool-like roofs, and the stop name and number picked out in mosaic tiles.

★ Top Tips

o You can buy art at numerous workshops around the neighborhood, including Fuster's own studio.

o For the best view of Fusterlandia, climb the observation tower inside Fuster's house.

o Allow time to stroll around the quieter streets of the neighborhood and meet some of its residents.

✕ Take a Break

Stroll 750m west to Santy Pescador (p122) for some of Havana's freshest seafood.

★ Getting There

🚗 A taxi from central Havana should cost US$15 to US$20.

🚌 Take Havana Bus Tour T1 service from Parque Central to La Cecilia in Playa and change to bus T2 (it doesn't always run so check ahead). Get off at the Gaudí-esque bus stop on Av 5.

Worth a Trip Embrace the Avant-Garde at Fusterlandia

Explore ◈
Playas del Este

Habana del Este is home to Playas del Este, a multi-flavored if slightly unkempt beach strip situated 18km east of Habana Vieja. While the beaches here are sublime, the accompanying resorts aren't exactly luxurious. But for those who dislike modern tourist development or are keen to see how Cubans get out and enjoy themselves, Playas del Este is a breath of fresh (sea) air.

The Short List

○ **Beaches (p132)** *Soaking up a rainbow of atmospheres on Havana's glorious eastern beaches.*

○ **Tarará (p135)** *Heading to Havana's eastern marina for diving and other water sports.*

○ **Los Chinos Pizza (p135)** *Decamping to the beach strip's east end for Neapolitan-style pizza in diminutive Guanabo.*

○ **Cojímar (p136)** *Diverting to this small fishing village where Hemingway once downed a cocktail or six.*

○ **Ajiaco Café (p139)** *Learning the secrets of comida cubana in Havana's premier farm-to-table restaurant.*

Getting There & Around

🚌 Habana Bus Tour's T3 bus runs every 40 minutes from Parque Central to Playa Santa María del Mar – pay by credit card on the bus. Local bus A40 stops at the roundabout at Calle 462 and Av 5 in Guanabo before heading into Havana.

🚗 A taxi from Centro Habana to Playas del Este costs between US$15 and US$20.

Playas del Este Map on p134

Playa El Mégano (p133) TUPUNGATO/SHUTTERSTOCK ©

Walking Tour 🥾

Havana's Eastern Beaches

Havana's eastern beaches stretch for 8km in an unbroken line from Tarará in the west to Guanabo in the east. While none of the strip carries the tourist-heavy all-inclusive atmosphere of Varadero, each parcel of sand retains a distinct flavor, from LGBTIQ+ friendly Boca Ciega to the uncensored local scene of Guanabo.

Walk Facts
Start Playa Tarará
End Guanabo Village
Length 8km; 3½ hours

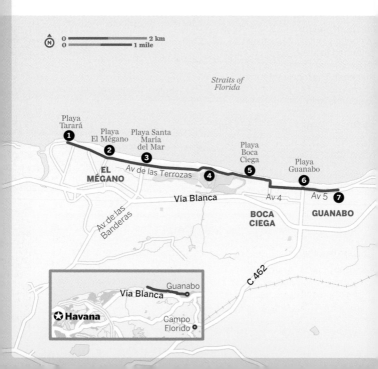

❶ Playa Tarará

The home of one of Havana's two marinas, Tarará supports its own resort village, a sprawling cluster of 1960s holiday bungalows still used mostly by Cuban vacationers. Plush it isn't, although the adjacent beach is pretty and relatively quiet in low season. Known for its ocean whitecaps, the area is an under-the-radar kiteboarding nexus.

❷ Playa El Mégano

El Mégano, where the fun starts, is popular enough to justify its own *punto náutico* (stand renting out beach toys), but sufficiently detached to avoid the screaming reggaeton sometimes heard further east. The local restaurant can arrange to bring your lunch out to you on the sand.

❸ Playa Santa María del Mar

Playas del Este's three main beach hotels line Playa Santa María del Mar, a high-quality stretch of sand protected by low dunes and shaded by occasional stands of palms. Various *punto náuticos* rent out beach kayaks, banana boats and other water toys.

❹ Laguna Itabo

A swampy lake surrounded by mangroves, this small lagoon sits just behind the dunes at the eastern end of Santa María del Mar. The best public access is via a wooden restaurant set on stilts above the water that was rebuilt in 2023.

❺ Playa Boca Ciega

The dunes get higher as you approach Boca Ciega, a broad beach abutting a small river mouth and lagoon. Since the 1990s this has been known as Havana's unofficial LGBTIQ+ beach, although with a nearby hotel you'll likely see as many straight as same-sex couples.

❻ Playa Guanabo

Backed by the small, scruffy beach town of Guanabo, this eastern stretch is a little stonier and not as well-maintained as the others. The bonus is the lively town that abuts it. While there's no fancy promenade, you'll encounter local life aplenty.

❼ Guanabo Village

Low-rise Guanabo, in contrast to the cheap-hotel zone further west, is a bona fide Cuban village, vibrating with an array of shops, bars and restaurants. The clip-clop of horse hooves provides a pleasant soundtrack and a meal at Los Chinos Pizza (p135) – considered by some *habaneros* to have the best thin-crust pizza in the city – is a fitting end to a sun-and-sand day.

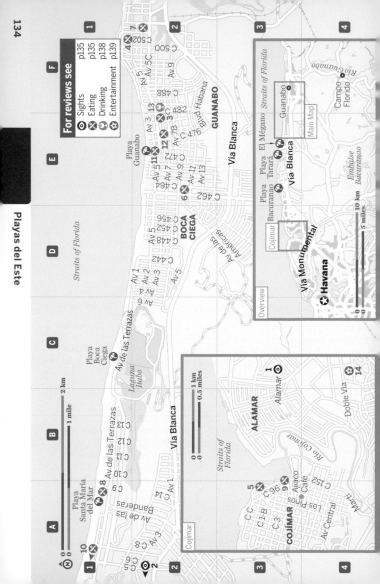

Playas del Este

For reviews see

⊗ Sights	p135
⊗ Eating	p135
⊖ Drinking	p138
⊕ Entertainment	p139

Straits of Florida

Playa Santa María del Mar

Playa Boca Ciega

Laguna Itabo

Av de las Terrazas

Av de las Banderas

Av de las Terrazas

Playa Guanabo

GUANABO

BOCA CIEGA

Bahía Habana

Vía Blanca

Av de las Américas

Straits of Florida

ALAMAR

Alamar

COJIMAR

Río Cojímar

Ajiaco Café

Los Pinos

Martí

Av Central

Doble Vía

Overview

Havana

Vía Monumental

Cojímar

Playa Bacuranao

Playa Tararará

Playa El Mégano

Straits of Florida

Guanabo

Vía Blanca

Vía Blanca

Embalse Bacuranao

Río Guanabo

Campo Florido

Main Map

Sights

Alamar AREA

1 MAP P134, C3

East across the river from Cojímar is a large housing estate of prefabricated apartment blocks constructed from 1971 by *micro brigadas* (small armies of workers who built post-revolution housing). This is the birthplace of Cuban rap, and an annual hip-hop festival is centered here. It is also the home of one of Cuba's largest and most successful urban agricultural gardens, the Organopónico Vivero Alamar.

Marlin Náutica Tarará WATER SPORTS

2 MAP P134, A2

Yacht charters, deep-sea fishing and scuba diving are offered at Marina Tarará, 22km east of Havana, although services can be sporadic. It's generally best to check ahead at a hotel tour desk in Havana before heading out. Prices are similar to those at Marina Hemingway. (cubanautica.travel/en/destinos/la-habana)

Eating

Los Chinos Pizza PIZZA $

3 MAP P134, E2

Established, no doubt, with large consortiums of visiting Italians in mind, these Guanabo-based pizza shapers know their stuff, cooking their well-loaded pies

Beach Toys

There are a number of **Club Náutica** points spaced along the beaches. The most central is outside Club Atlántico in the middle of Playa Santa María del Mar. Here you can rent pedal boats, banana boats, one-/two-person kayaks, snorkel gear and catamarans. A paddle around the coast exploring the mangrove-choked canals is a pleasure. Rates are displayed on large sandwich boards.

The points also rent sun loungers and parasols and can arrange for food from local restaurants to be brought out to you on the beach.

in a brick-lined, wood-fire oven from where they emerge looking refreshingly Neapolitan. There's simple alfresco seating and quick-fire service.

Il Piccolo ITALIAN $$

4 MAP P134, F1

This Guanabo private restaurant has been around for eons and is an open secret among *habaneros*, some of whom consider its thin-crust wood-oven pizzas to be the best in Cuba. Out of the way and a little more expensive than Playas del Este's other numerous pizza joints, it's well worth the journey (take a horse and cart along Av 5). (7-796-4300)

Donde Albert
CUBAN $$

5 MAP P134, A3

A homey family-run place within fishing distance of the ocean and next to Cojímar's small fort. One imagines Hemingway would have loved it here – a large painting of him adorns the patio as if to prove it and is surrounded by other sea-faring paraphernalia. Food, especially the fish, is from homemade heaven and there's a wonderful cake shop next door.

Restaurante 421
CUBAN $$

6 MAP P134, E2

Ask a local where to eat in Guanabo and they'll probably direct you up the gentle hill behind the main roundabout to this pleasant perch that has a surprisingly wide selection of Cuban favorites, mixed with international dishes such as paella, rabbit and the inevitable pizza. Sit on the windy patio and enjoy cheap lobster while shooting the breeze with the waitstaff. (5-305-6900)

Chicken Little
INTERNATIONAL $$

7 MAP P134, F2

Forgive it the kitschy name – Chicken Little could yet make it big. Defying Guanabo's ramshackle image, this clean-cut restaurant has polite waitstaff with welcome cocktails who'll talk you through a menu of pesto chicken, chicken in orange-and-honey sauce, and at least a dozen other dishes (some of which don't even involve chicken!). (7-796-2351)

Hemingway's Cojímar

Situated 10km east of Havana is the little port town of Cojímar, famous for harboring Ernest Hemingway's fishing boat *El Pilar* in the 1940s and '50s. These days it's an obligatory stop on any 'Hemingway-wos-'ere' tour, with groups arriving primarily to visit the historic restaurant, La Terraza de Cojímar where Ernesto once sank daiquiris.

Overlooking Cojímar's harbor is an old Spanish **fort** dating from 1649, a twin of the Torreón de la Chorrera in Vedado. It was the first fortification taken by the British when they attacked Havana from the rear in 1762. Until recently, the tower was used by the Cuban coast guard. However, there are plans to renovate it in the future.

Next to the tower and framed by a neoclassical archway is a gilded **bust** of Hemingway, erected by the residents of Cojímar in 1962 with his birthdate wrongly listed as 1898.

La Terraza de Cojímar

Don Pepe
SEAFOOD $$

8  MAP P134, A1

When the Guanabo pizza gets too much, head to this thatched-roof, beach-style restaurant about 50m from the sands of Playa Santa María del Mar. It specializes in seafood.

La Terraza de Cojímar
SEAFOOD $$

9  MAP P134, A3

Another shrine to the ghost of Hemingway, La Terraza special-izes in seafood and does a roaring trade with the hordes of Papa fans who are bused in daily. The food is surprisingly mediocre, although the terrace dining room overlooking the bay is pleasant. More atmospheric is the old bar out front, where mojito prices haven't yet reached El Floridita levels. (📞7-766-5151)

Cafetería El Mégano
CUBAN $

10  MAP P134, A1

It doesn't look much from the outside but the best thing about this diminutive place on Playa El Mégano is that it'll bring out its filling rice-and-beans-laced meals for you to enjoy on the beach – table, chairs and all. You barely have to move off your sun lounger; just place your order with one of the señores at the nearby *punto naútico* and they'll do the rest.

La Casa Quinta
CUBAN $

11  MAP P134, E2

Local streetside restaurant under private ownership that doesn't stray far from the Cuban classics, which it fires off quickly and cheaply with minimal drama. It's on Av 5, hence the name, and handily close to the beach. You can't go wrong with the grilled fish.

Pan.com
CAFE $

12 MAP P134, E2

It's cheap, it's state-run and it's pretty gritty inside, but this Cuban fast-food joint in Guanabo lures in locals with hot sandwiches on wonderful crusty Cuban bread that crumbles all over the table when you bite into it. Round off proceedings with a creamy milkshake and you'll be more than ready for a hard day at the beach.

Drinking

Bar Kopas
BAR

13 MAP P134, F2

With its luminous interior and open terrace overlooking the street, Kopas sports a street-level BBQ restaurant but is equally popular for its drinks and night-time action upstairs. This being Guanabo, you can expect to see plenty of foreign men of a certain age and their Cuban companions.

Cojimar (p136)

Farm-to-Table
Ajiaco Café ｜◯｜

There are, arguably, two reasons to come to suburban Cojimar: first, to pursue the ghost of Ernest Hemingway and, second, to visit this farm-to-table **restaurant** (Map p134, A4; cafeajiaco@gmail.com; 📝) named for a quintessential Cuban stew that headlines a menu of Cuban classics, all executed with rustic creativity.

Here you can order fried chickpeas, pork ribs in a barbecue-and-honey sauce, or a unique shredded-beef-and-plantain pizza. Service in the open-sided country-style restaurant is exceptional, and the smooth coffee might just be the finest in Cuba.

Best of all, Ajiaco offers **cooking classes** (US$50) that involve a visit to a nearby *finca* (farm) to choose ingredients, followed by time to prep, cook and eat your selected concoction back at the restaurant. Classes run daily if there are enough people.

Entertainment

Centro Cultural
Enguayabera   ARTS CENTER

14 ⭐ MAP P134, C4

In an old shirt factory abandoned in the 1990s, when it became a rubbish dump and public urinal, this state-sponsored community arts project in Alamar was inspired by the Fábrica de Arte Cubano (p106) in Vedado. Numerous funky venues are bivouacked under its cultural umbrella, including three small cinemas, a literary cafe, a theater and a crafts outlet.

Worth a Trip 👀

Explore a Literary Legacy at Museo Hemingway

📞 7-692-0176

Cuba wasn't just a passing dalliance for American writer Ernest Hemingway. The well-traveled novelist lived in the Finca la Vigía in the tranquil Havana suburb of San Francisco de Paula for over two decades, starting in 1939. When he departed for the US in 1960 soon after the Castro revolution, his house was taken over by the Cuban government and later made into a museum.

La Casona

The main attraction at the so-called Museo Hemingway is the house itself, an attractive single-story abode full of natural light and open, spacious rooms. To prevent the pilfering of objects, visitors are not allowed inside, but there are enough open doors and windows to allow a candid glimpse of Papa's unusual universe. Not surprisingly, there are books everywhere (including beside the toilet), a large Victrola and record collection, and an alarming number of animal heads.

La Torre

The three-story tower next to the main house was where the author came to relax, ruminate and sometimes write. It contains a tiny typewriter, a telescope, a comfortable lounger and plenty of dusty books. The view north toward the distant city is suitably inspiring.

The Pool & Pérgola

You'll need to use a little imagination to refill Hemingway's elegant swimming pool with water and summon up the ghost of actress Ava Gardner swimming naked in it. Alternatively, you can just collapse onto a chaise longue and enjoy the whispering palms and the craning bamboo. Two bathhouses either side of the traditional *pérgola* contain interesting photos of Hemingway and his guests enjoying booze and book talk by the pool.

Pilar

El Pilar was Hemingway's beloved wooden fishing boat that he once kept moored at the nearby village of Cojímar. Today it sits in dry dock next to the swimming pool on the site of the writer's former tennis court. Nearby is an erstwhile baseball diamond and cock-fighting ring.

★ Top Tips

o Don't come if it's raining, as most sights are outdoors and sometimes close in inclement weather.

o For full Hemingway immersion you can partake in a Hemingway tour. Most Havana agencies offer trips that take in the museum along with many of the writer's favorite drinking holes.

✗ Take a Break

The museum complex has its own small **cafeteria**, selling mainly drinks. Make the most of it; there's little else to whet the appetite in these parts.

★ Getting There

🚍 The P-7 metro bus from Parque de la Fraternidad in Centro Habana stops on the main road just outside the museum. Bus P-2 uses the same stop and runs to and from Vedado.

Survival Guide

Habana Vieja (p35) BIM/GETTY IMAGES ©

Before You Go

Book Your Stay

o With literally thousands of casas particulares (private houses) letting rooms, you'll never struggle to find accommodations in Havana.

o Rock-bottom budget hotels can equal casas for price but not comfort.

o There's a growing number of privately run 'boutique' hotels and a surge of new top-end places built by the state and part-run by foreign chains such as Blue Diamond, Kempinski and Iberostar. While they offer plenty of atmosphere, they can't match facilities elsewhere in the Caribbean.

Useful Websites

o **Cuba Casas** (cubacasas.net) Canadian-based website in English and French with hundreds of regularly updated casas particulares listings and photos.

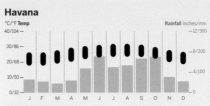

Havana
°C/°F Temp
Rainfall inches/mm

When to Go

o **Feb** Peak season

o **Aug–Oct** Hot but fun, especially if you're here for Carnaval. Come in October to avoid the summer heat and still have plenty to do.

o **Dec** Busy, with people lining up for the film festival.

o **Casa Particular Organization** (casaparticularcuba.org) Comprehensive listings of Cuba's private homestays.

o **A Nash Travel** (nashtravel.com) Long-standing Canada-based travel agency that can book any hotel in the city.

o **Lonely Planet** (lonelyplanet.com/cuba/hotels) Recommendations and bookings.

Best Budget

o **Hostal Peregrino Consulado** (hostalperegrino.com) Friendly and charming cross between a European guesthouse and a backpackers' hostel.

o **Residencia Albero Dulce** (alberodulce.com) Super-comfortable casa near the Plaza de la Revolución that also offers cooking classes, yoga and tours in classic American cars.

o **Hostal Neptuno 1915** (facebook.com/hostalneptuno1915) Seven delightful rooms, adorned with original art, elegant furniture and deluxe modern bathrooms, surrounding a small 1st-floor patio and reception-lounge.

o **Casa 1932** (casa1932.com) A private rental dedicated to the age of art deco that offers epic breakfasts.

Best Midrange

○ El Candil Boutique Hotel (hotelcandil.com) The mark of a trend, this private boutique hotel is setting a high bar.

○ Boutique Hotel 5tay8 Vedado (5tay8vedado.com) Effortlessly mixing art, luxury, old and new in Vedado's emerging grid.

○ Casavana Cuba (casavanacuba.com) The king of Havana's casas particulares is a bit pricey, but worth it.

○ Hotel Claxon (claxonhotel.com) Super modern boutique-style rooms in an elegant eclectic villa in Vedado that incorporates one of Havana's best restaurants.

Best Top End

○ Malecón 663 (malecon663.com) A piece of art on Havana's blustery sea drive with rooms as inspirational as they are comfortable.

○ Hotel Royalton Habana (royaltonresorts. com/resorts/habana) The best of Havana's five-stars hogs the prime real estate on the

corner of Prado and the Malecón.

○ Hotel Iberostar Parque Central (iberostar.com) Multiple facilities and sharp service at this centrally located five-star.

○ Gardens (gardens havana.com) The epitome of shabby-chic in Habana Vieja, Gardens is a beautifully decorated four-bedroom boutique hotel with handmade furniture and a rooftop pool.

Arriving in Havana

Aeropuerto Internacional José Martí

○ Aeropuerto Internacional José Martí (Av Rancho Boyeros) is at Rancho Boyeros, 20km southwest of Havana via Av de la Independencia. There are four terminals.

○ Public transportation from the airport into central Havana is practically nonexistent. A standard taxi will cost you approximately

US$30 and take 30 to 40 minutes to reach most of the city center hotels. You can change money at the bank outside the arrivals hall.

Terminal Sierra Maestra

○ Cruise ships arrive at a terminal in Havana harbor right on the edge of Habana Vieja. At the time of research, no American ships were calling at Cuban ports.

La Coubre Train Station

○ Cuba's train network (with most services converging on Havana) is extensive but traditionally not well-maintained. Things improved a little in 2019 with the introduction of carriages from China along with updated schedules for many routes.

○ Trains to most parts of Cuba depart from La Coubre station (Estación Central de Ferrocarriles is being refurbished until 2023 or later). La Coubre is on the southwestern side of Habana Vieja.

Terminal de Ómnibus

o Víazul (viazul.com) covers most destinations of interest to travelers, in safe, air-conditioned coaches.

o Services depart from a terminal 3.5km from central Havana. Víazul buses run to practically every town of interest to tourists.

Getting Around

Bus

o The handy hop-on, hop-off **Habana Bus Tour** runs on two main routes: T1 and T3.

o The main stop is in Parque Central opposite the Hotel Inglaterra. This is the pickup point for bus T1, which runs from Habana Vieja via Centro Habana, the Malecón, Calle 23 and Plaza de la Revolución to La Cecilia at the western end of Playa; and bus T3, which runs from Centro Habana to Playas del Este (via Parque Histórico Militar Morro-Cabaña).

Bike

o Several reputable companies in Havana hire out bikes that are fine for getting around town. **Ruta Bikes** (rutabikes. com) are probably the most reliable option.

o If you're uncertain of the geography or the slightly manic road rules, take a guided tour first.

Taxi

o Taxis hang around in front of all the major tourist hotels, outside the two main bus stations and at various city-center nexus points such as Parque Central and Parque de la Fraternidad. You're never far from a taxi in Havana.

o The most common taxis are the yellow cabs of **Cubataxi**, which are generally modern, air-conditioned and fitted with meters – but they also cost more.

o Cheaper are the legal private taxis. These cars are often yellow-and-black Ladas from the 1980s. You've got more chance haggling here, but agree on the fare before getting into the car. Private taxis will usually accept foreign currency including euros and US dollars.

Essential Information

Accessible Travel

o Cuba's inclusive culture extends to travelers with disabilities, and while facilities may be lacking, the generous nature of Cubans generally compensates when it can.

o With battered buses, potholed sidewalks and poorly maintained buildings, some of which haven't been renovated since the 1950s, independent travel can be difficult for people with physical disabilities.

o Many older buildings in Cuba don't have elevators or, if they do, they're regularly out of order. Similarly, public buses lack modifications for travelers with limited mobility. For comfort and reliability, modern Cubataxis are the best way of getting around.

o Steps and curbs are a perennial problem. Ramps are often not available or, when they are, can be steep.

o Only the more expensive hotels offer accessible rooms with wide doors and customized bathrooms. If it's your first time in Cuba, it might be better to invest in a higher-quality hotel that caters for travelers with disabilities. **Hotel Iberostar Parque Central** and **Gran Hotel Manzana Kempinski**, both in Parque Central, are good bets.

o Blind travelers will be helped across streets and given priority in lines. Etecsa phone centers have telephone equipment for deaf people, and TV programs are broadcast with closed captioning.

Business Hours

Banks 9am–3pm Monday to Friday

Cadeca money exchanges 9am–7pm Monday to Saturday, 9am–noon Sunday. Many top-end city hotels offer money exchange late into the evening.

Pharmacies 8am–8pm

Post offices 8am–5pm Monday to Saturday, sometimes longer

Restaurants Noon–midnight

Shops 9am–5pm Monday to Saturday, 9am–noon Sunday

Electricity

Type A
120V/60Hz

Type C
220V/50Hz

Emergencies

To call Cuba from abroad, dial your international access code, Cuba's country code, the city or area code (minus the '0,' which is used when dialing domestically between provinces), and the local number.

Cuba's country code	53
Emergency	106
Directory assistance	113
Police	106
Fire	105

Money

o Money continues to be the trickiest question for travelers contemplating a trip to Cuba with the situation changing regularly.

o After over a year of hyperinflation and the growth of a rampant black market, the Cuban government radically readjusted its exchange rate in August 2022, from 24 pesos to a US dollar to over 120 pesos to a US dollar.

o This is the rate you'll get if you change your money in government-run banks and Cadecas (exchange booths). You can check the current rates for all the main currencies on the Cadeca website (cadeca. cu/en).

o As it stands, the euro is the best foreign currency to bring to Cuba because it's the most widely accepted and subject to the lowest bank fees (approximately 2%). Furthermore, many private businesspeople (restaurateurs, taxi drivers, homestay owners) prefer to be paid directly in euros rather than Cuban pesos (although they'll accept both). Some state-run businesses also accept euros.

The Black Market

o Cuba has a huge informal black market and practically everyone is in on it. The unofficial 'on-the-street' exchange rate is invariably more favorable than the official government rate (ie the rate you'll be offered in banks, ATMs and Cadecas and when making credit card transactions).

o Never change money with a stranger on the street.

o Remember euros and US dollars are widely accepted in Cuba, but always check the exchange rate you're getting vis-à-vis pesos before using them.

ATMs

ATMs are now widespread in Havana and usually function pretty efficiently. Check with your home bank before your departure regarding your card's functionality in Cuba. Cuban ATMs generally accept non-US-linked Visa credit and debit cards. Machines dispatch Cuban pesos at the official exchange rate.

How to Change Money Safely

o Only change money in small amounts. Rates fluctuate constantly and you can't take excess pesos out of Cuba.

o Avoid changing money at the airport where the rates are poor.

o Cuba's currency rules are highly volatile. Check for updates before your trip.

o You can find the official exchange rates on cadeca.cu and bc.gob. cu. Approximate unofficial rates can be found on eltoque.com.

Dos & Don'ts

Cuba is an informal country with few rules of etiquette.

o **Greetings** Shake hands with strangers; a kiss or double-cheek kiss is appropriate between people (men–women and women–women) who have already met.

o **Conversation** Although they can be surprisingly candid, Cubans aren't keen to discuss politics, especially with strangers and if it involves being openly critical of the government.

o **Dancing** Cubans don't harbor any self-consciousness about dancing. Throw your reservations out the window and let loose.

Tours from the US

Although the Trump administration ended group people-to-people trips in 2019, several US companies have continued to offer licensed Cuba tours by re-registering under the US Department of the Treasury's 'support for the Cuban people' category. These include:

Cuba Travel Services (cubatravelservices.com) Great source of general travel information for US travelers. It also arranges flights, accommodations, car rental and travel packages.

GeoEx (geoex.com) Runs luxury people-to-people trips of six to eight days' duration from the US, plus opportunities to build your own custom trip. Tours can include everything from meeting economists to delving into Cuba's complex religious rites.

Insight Cuba (insightcuba.com) A well-established registered Cuba operator serving American travelers. Insight's trips include a one-week jazz-themed excursion and a trip to run the Havana marathon in November.

Road Scholar (roadscholar.org) The largest non-profit provider of learning adventures in Cuba, with several trips including birdwatching, community art projects and organic farm visits.

Credit Cards

Credit cards are accepted in Cuba – indeed, they are the *only* way to pay for some services, including rooms in state-run hotels, car rental, bus tickets and goods in state-run shops and restaurants. Credit cards affiliated to US banks are not accepted.

Tipping

Tipping in Cuba is important.

○ **Resorts/hotels** Around 10% for good service.

○ **Musicians** Small notes for restaurant musicians when the basket comes around.

○ **Tour guides** Depending on tour length (a dollar for a few hours, more for extensive guiding).

○ **Restaurants** Standard 10% (up to 15% for excellent service).

○ **Taxis** If on the meter 10%; otherwise, agree the full fare beforehand.

Public Holidays

Officially Cuba has 10 public holidays.

January 1 Triunfo de la Revolución (Liberation Day)

January 2 Día de la Victoria (Victory of the Armed Forces)

March/April (date varies) Good Friday

US Travelers & Cuba

Despite recent bans on cruise ships and 'people-to-people' trips, US citizens can still apply for a 'general license' to travel to Cuba under 12 different categories listed by the US Department of the Treasury. These range from the specific (public performances or athletic competitions) to the vague ('support for the Cuban people'). Independent travelers with no specific affiliations are best off qualifying under the 'support for the Cuban people' category, a relatively open classification.

General licenses are self-qualifying and require no long-winded paperwork. To avoid any legal ramifications when returning to the US, you are advised to draw up a detailed trip itinerary before you go and to keep all receipts and addresses of places where you stayed and visited for five years after your return.

Essential bedtime reading for all US citizens wishing to undertake travel to Cuba is the regularly updated fact sheet on the Department of the Treasury website: treasury.gov/resource-center/sanctions/Programs/pages/cuba.aspx.

May 1 Día de los Trabajadores (International Worker's Day)

July 25–27 Día de la Rebeldía Nacional (Commemoration of Moncada Attack)

October 10 Día de la Independencia (Independencia Day)

December 25 Navidad (Christmas Day)

December 31 New Year's Eve

Safe Travel

Havana is not a dangerous city, especially when compared to other metropolitan areas in North and South America. There's almost no gun crime, violent robbery, organized gang culture, teenage delinquency, drugs or dangerous no-go zones. Stiff prison sentences for crimes such as assault have acted as a major deterrent for would-be criminals and kept organized crime at bay. Things to be aware of as a traveler:

○ Petty theft and pickpocketing

○ Short-changing in bars and restaurants

○ Street hustlers selling cigars

○ For women, sexist banter and unwanted attention from men

Telephone Services

○ Cubacel has a wide range of roaming agreements. See the full list here: etecsa.cu/en/visitors/roaming.

○ You can use your own GSM or TDMA phone in Cuba with a local SIM card, though you'll need to ensure your phone is unlocked first. Buy a SIM card at an Etecsa *telepunto*. Bring your passport. There's an Etecsa office at Havana airport as well as two offices in town.

○ When all's said and done, to communicate with people abroad it may be cheaper to buy a charge-by-the-hour internet card, find a wi-fi signal and use Skype or WhatsApp.

Toilets

Havana isn't over-endowed with clean and accessible public toilets. Most tourists slip into upscale hotels if they're caught short. Even there, restrooms often lack toilet paper, soap and door locks.

You'll generally have to tip the toilet attendant.

Tourist Information

○ State-run **Infotur** (infotur.cu) books tours and has maps, phone cards and useful free brochures.

○ Pretty much every hotel in Havana has some type of state-run tourist-information desk.

Visas

○ Regular tourists who plan to spend up to two months in Cuba do not need visas. Instead, you get a *tarjeta de turista* (tourist card).

○ Package tourists receive their tourist card with their other travel documents. Those going 'air only' usually buy the tourist card from the travel agency or airline office that sells them the plane ticket, but policies vary (eg Canadian airlines give out tourist cards on their airplanes), so you'll need to check ahead with the airline office via phone or email. In some cases you may be required to buy and/or pick up the card at your departure airport, and sometimes at the flight gate itself some minutes before departure.

Language

Spanish pronunciation is pretty straightforward – Spanish spelling is phonetically consistent, meaning that there's a clear and consistent relationship between what you see in writing and how it's pronounced. Also, most Latin American Spanish sounds are pronounced the same as their English counterparts. Note though that the **kh** in our pronunciation guides is a throaty sound (like the 'ch' in the Scottish loch), **v** and **b** are similar to the English 'b' (but softer, between a 'v' and a 'b'), and **r** is strongly rolled. If you read our pronunciation guides as if they were English, you'll be understood just fine. The stressed syllables are in italics.

To enhance your trip with a phrasebook, visit: lonelyplanet.com.

Basics

Hello.	*Hola.*	o·la
Goodbye.	*Adiós.*	a·*dyos*
Sorry.	*Lo siento.*	lo *syen*·to
Yes./No.	*Sí./No.*	see/no
Please.	*Por favor.*	por fa·*vor*

How are you?
¿Qué tal?   ke tal

Fine, thanks.
Bien, gracias.   byen *gra*·syas

Excuse me.
Perdón.   per·*don*

Thank you.
Gracias.   *gra*·syas

You're welcome.
De nada.   de *na*·da

My name is ...
Me llamo ...   me *ya*·mo ...

What's your name?
¿Cómo se   *ko*·mo se
llama usted?   *ya*·ma oo·*ste* (pol)

Do you speak English?
¿Habla inglés?   a·bla een·*gles* (pol)

I don't understand.
Yo no entiendo.   yo no en·*tyen*·do

Eating & Drinking

What would you recommend?
¿Qué recomienda?   ke re·ko·*myen*·da

I don't eat ...
No como ...   no *ko*·mo ...

Please bring the bill.
Por favor nos trae   por fa·*vor* nos *tra*·e
la cuenta.   la *kwen*·ta

Cheers!
¡Salud!   sa·*loo*

I'd like to book a table for ...
Quisiera reservar   kee·*sye*·ra re·ser·*var*
una mesa para ...   oo·na me·sa *pa*·ra ...

   (eight) o'clock
   las (ocho)   las (o·cho)

   (two) people
   (dos) personas   (dos) per·so·nas

Shopping

How much is it?
¿Cuánto cuesta?   kwan·to kwes·ta

I'm just looking.
Sólo estoy   so·lo es·toy
mirando.   mee·ran·do

That's too expensive.
Es muy caro.   es mooy ka·ro

Can you lower the price?
¿Podría bajar   po·dree·a ba·khar
un poco el precio? oon po·ko el pre·syo

Emergencies

Help!   ¡Socorro!   so·ko·ro

Go away!   ¡Vete!   ve·te

Call ...!   ¡Llame a ...! ya·me a ...

   a doctor
   un médico   oon me·dee·ko

   the police
   la policía   la po·lee·see·a

I'm lost. (m/f)
Estoy perdido/a.   es·toy per·dee·do/a

I'm ill.
Estoy enfermo/a.   es·toy en·fer·mo/a

Where are the toilets?
¿Dónde están   don·de es·tan
los servicios?   los ser·vee·syos

Time & Numbers

morning	mañana	ma·nya·na
afternoon	tarde	tar·de
evening	noche	no·che
yesterday	ayer	a·yer
today	hoy	oy
tomorrow	mañana	ma·nya·na

1	uno	oo·no
2	dos	dos
3	tres	tres
4	cuatro	kwa·tro
5	çinço	seen·ko
6	seis	seys
7	siete	sye·te
8	ocho	o·cho
9	nueve	nwe·ve
10	diez	dyes

What time is it?
¿Qué hora es?   ke o·ra es

It's (10) o'clock.
Son (las diez).   son (las dyes)

It's half past (one).
Es (la una)   es (la oo·na)
y media.   ee me·dya

Transport & Directions

Where's ...?
¿Dónde está ...?   don·de es·ta ...

What's the address?
¿Cuál es   kwal es
la dirección?   la dee·rek·syon

I want to go to ...
Quisiera ir a ... kee·sye·ra eer a ...

Does it stop at ...?
¿Para en ...?   pa·ra en ...

What stop is this?
¿Cuál es esta   kwal es es·ta
parada?   pa·ra·da

What time does it arrive/leave?
¿A qué hora   a ke o·ra
llega/sale?   ye·ga/sa·le

Behind the Scenes

Send Us Your Feedback

We love to hear from travelers – your comments help make our books better. We read every word, and we guarantee that your feedback goes straight to the authors. Visit **lonelyplanet.com/contact** to submit your updates and suggestions.

Note: We may edit, reproduce and incorporate your comments in Lonely Planet products such as guidebooks, websites and digital products, so let us know if you are happy to have your name acknowledged. For a copy of our privacy policy visit **lonelyplanet.com/legal**.

Brendan's Thanks

Special thanks to all my many Cuban *amigos,* especially Julio & Elsa Roque at Hostal Peregrino, Luis Miguel Ulacia at Casa 1932, Osiris Oliver at El Rum Rum de la Habana, Titina in Playa and Celine in Vedado. An extra *gracias* to Carlos Sarmiento for his careful driving skills and excellent company and to my wife Liz and son Kieran for joining me on the road and (I think) enjoying it.

Acknowledgements

Cover photographs: (front) Classic car on Paseo de Martí, Susanne Kremer/4Corners Images ©; (back) Cuban musician playing a trumpet, Bim/Getty Images ©

Photographs pp30–31 (clockwise from top right): Vadim_N/Shutterstock ©; Tupungato/Shutterstock ©; Hemis/Alamy Stock Photo ©

This Book

This 2nd edition of Lonely Planet's *Pocket Havana* guidebook was researched and written by Brendan Sainsbury. The previous edition was also written by Brendan Sainsbury. This guidebook was produced by the following:

Destination Editor Alicia Johnson

Production Editor Sofie Andersen

Cartographer Julie Sheridan

Book Designer Virginia Moreno

Assisting Editors Anne Mulvaney, Mani Ramaswamy

Cover Researchers Gwen Cotter, Brendan Dempsey-Spencer

Thanks to Ronan Abayawickrema, Noémie Albert, James Appleton, Imogen Bannister, Jess Boland, Anna Carriero, Alex Davids, Jana DeLuna, Karen Henderson, Alison Killilea, Jasmine Stodel

Index

See also separate subindexes for:

- ❸ Eating p157
- ❺ Drinking p158
- ❻ Entertainment p158
- ❼ Shopping p158

Sights 000
Map Pages **000**

Our Writers

Brendan Sainsbury

Born and raised in the UK in a town that never merits a mention in any guidebook (Andover, Hampshire), Brendan spent the holidays of his youth caravanning in the English Lake District and didn't leave Blighty until he was nineteen. Making up for lost time, he's since squeezed 80 countries into a sometimes precarious existence as a writer and professional vagabond. In the last 18 years, he has written over 60 books for Lonely Planet from Castro's Cuba to the jungles of Colombia. When not scribbling research notes, Brendan likes partaking in ridiculous 'endurance' races, strumming old Clash songs on the guitar, and experiencing the pain and occasional pleasures of following Southampton Football Club.

Published by Lonely Planet Global Limited
CRN 554153
2nd edition – December 2023
ISBN 978 1 78701 375 9
© Lonely Planet 2023   Photographs © as indicated 2023
10 9 8 7 6 5 4 3 2 1
Printed in Malaysia